I SHALL NOT WANT

by

Elizabeth M. Boyd

Illustrations
by
Judy Guedes

Copyright © 2012
by Elizabeth M. Boyd Illustrations by Judy I. Guedes

I Shall Not Want
by Elizabeth M. Boyd Illustrations by Judy I. Guedes

Printed in the United States of America

ISBN 9781619965102

All rights reserved solely by the author. The author guarantees all contents are original and do not infringe upon the legal rights of any other person or work. No part of this book may be reproduced in any form without the permission of the author. The views expressed in this book are not necessarily those of the publisher.

Unless otherwise indicated, Bible quotations are taken from the Spirit Filled Life Bible NKJV. Copyright © 1991 by Thomas Nelson Inc., Nashville, Tennessee, USA.

www.xulonpress.com

Psalm 23:1-6, Spirit Filled Life Bible, NKJV, Thomas Nelson Publishers, Nashville, TN. USA, 1991.

FORWARD FROM THE EDITOR

Elizabeth and I have been friends for a number of years since I returned to Salt Spring Island in 1989. When I first met her, she handed me her book, I read it and didn't feel I understood it well enough to edit it. So we put it aside for a few years. By that time, I had gone through enough tough spots in my life that I felt perhaps I understood it, so I agreed to make another attempt.

I am only the vehicle that God has used to help put on paper this message that He gave to Elizabeth so many years ago.

I thank Elizabeth and God for giving me a second chance to be part of this project.

Judy Guedes.

INTRODUCTION
(M. LeGrand And Miss Petite)

The little sheep often walked
Beside the big sheep because
She enjoyed his company.
His conversation was interesting,
He cared for the little sheep,
And he would never have let
Harm befall her.

However, one day she fell ill,
And she knew there was nothing
She could do to help herself.
She struggled beside M. LeGrand
Not wanting to give in one moment
To her sickness.

"Here, Miss Petite. Sit here,"
M. LeGrand spoke quietly,
Trying to comfort the little sheep.
"I will go for the Shepherd,
He is the only one who can help you."
M. LeGrand didn't understand
The nature of her illness;
He just knew it was serious.

Without a word, Miss Petite lay down beside the path,
Obedient to M. LeGrand's command.
The grass was green and soft where she lay,
Waiting for the Shepherd.

"Dear Shepherd! Help! Dear Shepherd!"
M. LeGrand called though he was far away from
The Shepherd standing on top of the knoll.

When the Shepherd heard the cries for help,
He turned and ran to meet him.
M. LeGrand explained about Miss Petite
And the Shepherd understood immediately.

I Shall Not Want

I Shall Not Want

The Shepherd lifted her carefully in His strong arms
And carried her to the grassy knoll.
He found it necessary to shear Miss Petite's wool
Because of its extreme weight.
With the burden removed,
She could now run and play and dance
As she had always dreamed she would do.
The Shepherd knew her well, and what she needed.

Rather than return her to the flock,
Or even beside M. LeGrand,
The Shepherd chose to keep Miss Petite close
To Himself.

"My Dear Shepherd," Miss Petite pleaded.
"Would you allow me to return to the big sheep?
I miss him so much
And so want to walk by his side."

The Shepherd was a little hesitant
Explaining that the black sheep
Was very big compared to her,
And she may not be able to keep up.
Knowing all things, however,
The Shepherd allowed Miss Petite her wish,
And she ran as fast as she could to the big sheep.

"Big sheep! M. LeGrand! Black sheep!" she called, stumbling,
Trying to get the big sheep's attention.

It seemed like it had been forever
Since they had been together,
But now they continued their walk
At the rear of the flock.

Chapter 1

THE FLUTE

Miss Petite stood near the Shepherd.
A sweet, thin sound tickled her ear.
To go, to stay;
She enquired of the Shepherd;
"May I go?" she asked, excitedly.
"Yes," He cautioned, "but you are still
Too tired and weak to go far.
There is no need to run to find the flute.
Eventually, it will come to you where you are."

"Can the others not hear?" she puzzled.
"Can they not hear the flute?
Does it not stir them?"
The remaining flock walked, heads down,
Crunching as they ate.

Without hesitation, M. LeGrand
Started towards the music.
He looked at Miss Petite from the corner of his eye,
Catching a glimpse of her excitement.
It hadn't occurred to him to ask her to join him.
A tear trickled down her face
As she sought the Shepherd for consolation.

"Well, come on if you're coming", M. LeGrand said,
Stopping as quickly as he had started.
Delighted, Miss Petite leapt for joy,
And cantered down the path
With him to find the flute.

She leapt two, three and four steps
To keep pace with M. LeGrand.
Weariness overcame her
Until she sat on the side of the path and wept.
Aware of her weakness,
M. LeGrand helped her find a resting spot
Where she could stay until his return to the pasture.

She wasn't so disappointed
That she could not continue to find the music,
For the Shepherd assured her it would come to the pasture.
But she was disappointed in herself
That she kept M. LeGrand from reaching his destiny.

She was not afraid of being alone.
She slept so soundly that she had no idea
How much time had passed.
M. LeGrand arrived
With the music following closely behind.
Together, they returned to the flock.

Miss Petite leapt and bounced
Trying to tell the others in the flock
That the music was coming,
But the sheep ignored her.
They continued to munch, walk,
Heads down; they were just rude!

"Why do they not care about the music?"
She asked the Shepherd.

"Some are not interested,
Some don't want their eating disturbed,
Some have heard the music before
And are disappointed,
And some just do not enjoy flute music," He said.

"Please! Can't you make them listen?" asked Miss Petite.

"I can only give them all an opportunity to hear;
I cannot force them to listen," the Shepherd said lovingly.

The penetrating strains of the flute came closer;
M. LeGrand could not contain himself.
He began to dance, turning cartwheels.
He sang and clapped his hooves together,
Jumping for joy.
He picked up Miss Petite
And danced with her in circles.

I Shall Not Want

Chapter 2

THE BELL

The little sheep stared in amazement
At the bell, scratched and dulled with age.
It was attached to a worn leather strap,
Around the big sheep's neck, with a buckle
That was held with tarnished silver clasps.
Why hadn't she noticed it before?
It must have been there all the time.
"Are you aware of a bell around big sheep's neck?
What is it there for?" she asked the Shepherd timidly.

The Shepherd laughed.
"When the sheep were young,
I put bells on some of their necks
Because they wandered away.
With bells, I could hear where they were and find them easily."

"Did the big sheep wander away,
Or get lost? Is that why he has a bell?" Miss Petite queried.
"Did You put the bell on his neck?"

The Shepherd laughed heartily.
"Sometimes he went off on his own,
Thinking he was out of my sight;
But he never really was.
Do you remember when M. LeGrand
Told you that the Shepherd always knows
Where every one of His sheep is?
The big sheep learned that lesson when he was smaller
And never forgot it.
He knows I see him."

"And I see you", the Shepherd went on.
"Even when you think you are hiding beside him.
I know where all my sheep are.
If I don't see them, then I hear them by their bells
And I can find them quite readily."

"Then why, if he has learned his lesson,
Does he still have a bell?" she asked

"Sit, little one. I have a story to tell you," said the Shepherd.
"When M. LeGrand was just a little sheep himself,
He watched the bigger sheep in the flock.
He wanted to grow up to be like them someday.

I Shall Not Want

I Shall Not Want

Some sheep started to wander;
Others followed them;
So I called each one of them to Me
And placed a bell around the neck
Of each sheep who had gone astray;
The rebellious ones
Received larger bells.
M. LeGrand's fascination for bells was more than he could stand.
I set the basket of bells closer to him
And asked him to choose one.
Delighted, he picked one;
Bright brass, shiny and new."

The Shepherd smiled slightly.
"I knew he was too young to realize
He should be embarrassed to wear a bell
Because it was used as a control method
For those who liked to go their own way.

I took a special leather strap
And placed silver studs around it
That sparkled in the sun,
And in the moonlight!
When the young sheep put on the bell
He turned his head, lifted it up and down,
Walked, ran and trotted to make the bell
Play its music.

He was the only sheep who actually wanted one,
And the first to hear its music.

All the others wore their bells
But their ears were deaf
To their own bell
And to their neighbor's.
The bells were there for My benefit."

"Does the big sheep not play his bell anymore?" she said.

I Shall Not Want

The Shepherd looked sad, disheartened.
"No, the big sheep hasn't played his bell for a long time.
He rings it to see if it is still there,
Or to remind others he still has it.
He rings it when he is angry;
But he doesn't play it anymore."

Feeling she shouldn't press the subject further,
Miss Petite changed direction slightly.
"Why is his bell scratched and dirty?
Why wouldn't he let You
Shine up the bell, at least?" puzzled the little sheep.

"It is dull with age and use.
I have told him he could have a larger, shinier bell,
But he wished to keep the one
Of his youth.
The older M. LeGrand got, the less he trusted Me.
He was afraid I would take the bell and not return it.
He could have had any bell he wanted.
Until he believes Me,
And trusts Me,
I cannot change it for him," the Shepherd said.

"Perhaps I should go and persuade the big sheep
To trade his old bell for bells of different sizes!" Miss Petite insisted.

"May I have a bell around my neck;
Not large like the big sheep's bell, but something very small?
May I have it now, to show the big sheep and encourage him
To get his own bell cleaned or exchanged?" pleaded Miss Petite.

The Shepherd promised that she could have a tiny bell soon.
"Go now, my little one.
Wait. I will give it to you in time."

He loved the little sheep's innocence.
He loved M. LeGrand's steadiness.
He was faultless and strong.
Why wouldn't he trust the Shepherd more?
He never talked over his problems with the Shepherd.
He just trudged along,
Muddling through things by himself.

"The little sheep will never be like that.
She always needs a Shepherd," the Shepherd mused.

Chapter 3

ON BEING DIFFERENT

Miss Petite faced M. LeGrand
As one of the flock.
She talked amongst the sheep about their bells.
Some were happy with their bells;
Others were annoyed, even disgusted.
Some had never heard the music in their bells
While others heard them faintly but didn't care.
A few loved the sound that their bells made.
But none loved their bells as much as M. LeGrand loved his.

Some sheep took advantage of Miss Petite,
Using her to get their point across to M. LeGrand
Because they knew she spent much time with him.
Some things they had to say were constructive;
Some were not.
Were they not all of the same flock?
Had they not grown up together with him,
And played their bells together?
A few whispered, warning her
Not to spend too much time with M. LeGrand.
It would make others jealous.
He was, after all, a different kind of sheep.
Miss Petite was confused.

"What do you mean by a different kind of sheep?"
Miss Petite had never noticed anything different.
One sheep in front, overhearing the conversation,
Snorted over his shoulder,
"His horns are stupid! Haven't you noticed his horns?"

For the first time, Miss Petite realized
That M. LeGrand did have horns.
He had accidentally hit her with them
When she got too close to his head!
"How could I not have noticed that he was different from me?"
"Why didn't the Shepherd tell me he was different?" she thought.

Miss Petite backed away quietly from the flock.
And headed for the pasture
Where she collapsed,
Hurt, disheartened
And unsure of her feelings.

M. LeGrand felt a shift in the air;
Out of the corner of his eye,
He thought he saw two sheep whispering;
Perhaps glancing in his direction.
He moved away from the flock
Toward Miss Petite,
Not cautiously edging on the outside,
But boldly striding across the pasture.
"What are you doing away from the flock?" she asked.

M. LeGrand did not answer, just snuggled close.
"Do they upset you with the things they say about us?" he said.

Miss Petite was shocked
How did he know? He was so wise! she thought.
More at ease, she began to tell him
About the whisperings in the pasture,
But never mentioned the bell around
M. LeGrand's neck.

"I never noticed you were different from me.
Why didn't the Shepherd tell me?" said Miss Petite.
Why didn't you tell me we were different?"

"Has the Shepherd ever been upset that we have walked together?" he said.

"I was ashamed. I enjoyed having you beside me.
But I also tried to warn you not to get too close;
That you should spend more time in the pasture.
Do you remember when I butted your head accidentally?" said the big sheep.
"Do you recall what I was telling you at the time?"

"No. I was so hurt, so wounded, that I went back to the pasture,
And didn't even hear what you said to me!"
Miss Petite's voice was almost inaudible.

"It was for your own good.
I didn't want you to be ostracized from the flock!" M. LeGrand said quietly.

She didn't care what others thought.
She liked M. LeGrand and wanted to stay with him.

"See? They are even looking at us now as we talk here in the pasture.
Even with the Shepherd in plain view.
What do you think they would say
If you continued to walk beside me?" said the big black sheep.

"First you thought I was a nuisance;
Now I am different and that is why we can't walk together!" cried Miss Petite.

"I am sorry you don't understand;
I am sincerely concerned that the other sheep will not accept you
If we walk together much longer," M. LeGrand sighed.
"Let's be more discreet. You must go now."

As M. LeGrand started back to the flock, he turned to wave goodbye,
But Miss Petite was already running over to the Shepherd.
M. LeGrand shook his head and continued towards his flock.

"You seem upset. Was the big sheep offended
Over some comment about the bell?" inquired the Shepherd.

"Oh! The bell! I forgot all about the bell!" gasped Miss Petite.
She went over all the details, word for word;
The sheep comments, their likes and dislikes;
And their dislike for bells;
The looks, grunts and dirty details.
She aired her feelings too, asking the Shepherd's advice.
"I want to walk beside the big sheep,
Or even walk a step behind,
But I want to be close.
I could learn from him.
He is secure, comfortable,
Safe and warm."

The Shepherd again sat down beside Miss Petite,
Never tiring of explaining things to her.
"What if you were to get up on the knoll
And requested the attention of the other sheep?"

"They would laugh at me," she chuckled.

"Why would they laugh?" He asked.

The answers came easily, and she began to list them.
"I am younger than most;
I have been sick and so have not pulled my weight.
I have been groomed and fed by You,
Because I haven't been able to look after myself.
How could I expect to tell them anything?"
"Correct. And is there another reason, little sheep?" the Shepherd coaxed.

She knew He knew the answer, so she continued.
"There would be some who wouldn't listen
Because they are jealous I spend so much time with M. LeGrand,
Or they don't approve of him because he is different."

"Would that matter to you?" the Shepherd said.

"No," she uttered quickly.

"What you have to say might be extremely important.
It may be a matter of life or death.
Why would you not want all to hear you?" He said.

Miss Petite was now ashamed,
Head lowered, eyes cast down.
Again, she had been taught a hard lesson.

"Now, suppose I told you to speak a message
To this flock, and I told you what to say?
Would they listen?" the Shepherd, gently touched her head.

"Yes, without question, they'd listen,
Except, dear Shepherd,
For those who don't listen to You at any time.
There are some who do not listen to You even when You call them."

"Right you are, little sheep.
The sheep would listen because you speak in My Name.
It wouldn't matter to them that you have been weak and sickly.
They would know I had sent you,
That I would give you authority to speak to them;
That I would speak through you.
You would have no fear of any of them.
Shall we practice?" the Shepherd smiled.

"Can we bring the big sheep too, and try?"

"No," the Shepherd looked into her eyes directly.
"M. LeGrand is not ready to join you on the knoll.
Do you want to practice?"

"I don't know. I am frightened," she whimpered.

"You know I'd stay close to you, even right beside you,
And I would help you if you forgot some words," He reassured her.

"I'd feel so much better if the big sheep were here with me,
Or if You would let him go first," Miss Petite whined.
Miss Petite pleaded with the Shepherd
To let M. LeGrand come to stand beside her on the knoll
While she made her first speech;
Or behind her, a little out of sight;
At least present there for support.

The Shepherd agreed,
But Miss Petite saw something
Pass over the Shepherd's eye;
Like a mist
Or a veil
That came between them.

Miss Petite bounded off to tell M. LeGrand.
"The Shepherd is going to ask you to do something,
To make a speech, give a message at anytime
And you can join me on the knoll!
You won't have to do anything this time,
You will just be there for me, for moral support,
To help me get through this practice."

M. LeGrand stopped munching and turned quickly,
Almost bunting Miss Petite with his horns.
"Don't you realize what you have done to the Shepherd?
You don't need my support,
As long as you have the Shepherd there beside you,
Reminding you exactly what to say!"

Suddenly, the little sheep knew
That the veil in the Shepherd's eye
Was a hurt that she had put there.
She got sick to her stomach.

Without finishing her conversation with M. LeGrand,
Or mentioning the bell,
She slowly plodded her way to the Shepherd.
When she reached Him,
She bleated and pleaded with Him to forgive her
For hurting Him so much.

The Shepherd swept the little sheep
Up into His arms
And held her there for what seemed like
An eternity.

After some time,
The Shepherd put the little sheep
Down on the grass,
And told her to run along and play.
He assured her
She wouldn't be asked to speak
Or do anything until
The Shepherd knew for certain
That she was ready.
"Enjoy your time of fun,
Don't fret about what I might ask you to do.
Perhaps M. LeGrand
Might even be ready to join you by that time.
Good-bye, my little one."

It seemed strange that the Shepherd had said good-bye,
But she was so happy now.
She felt like a different sheep.
She could run, play and mingle with the other sheep;
Or walk alongside M. LeGrand..
She was free.
She could do anything;
The Shepherd had said it was so.

She wanted to see the big sheep, to share her happiness,
But she wasn't ready to get into heavy discussions with him.
There was so much of her talk with the Shepherd that she wanted to share,
But she didn't know if M. LeGrand would understand it.
Would it upset him, or would he even want to hear it?
Inside, she felt the big sheep might think her pompous
About the freedom she had to talk with the Shepherd.
Everything was new, fresh, and precious.
She couldn't let M. LeGrand, or anyone
Steal any of the joy.

Chapter 4

HAVE PATIENCE

For a long time, the two of them sang together
And laughed over silly little things.
Then the Shepherd put Miss Petite down.
She did not move.
The Shepherd waited for a response,
But there was none.
The little sheep wanted to talk about something
But was too embarrassed,
So she stayed there, next to the Shepherd.
She told Him she really didn't want to leave.
She wanted to stay beside Him and watch the sunset.

Actually, she could hardly wait for the sunset to disappear
So it would be dark.
She waited patiently, and when it was dark enough,
She slipped away without even saying goodnight to the Shepherd.
Miss Petite decided she'd spend the night in the pasture,
But not too close to the Shepherd.
She didn't want the other sheep to think she was still being
Cared for by Him.

She had only moved a short distance
When she heard the Shepherd call to her.
Oh, how she wanted to pretend
That she hadn't heard that call.

She didn't want that crook around her neck,
So she stopped, but didn't look back.
She waited.
The Shepherd came along side of Miss Petite.
"Would you like to talk to Me now, in the dark?"

"It is too late and chilly now," she said.
The Shepherd ignored her comments and started a fire.
Oh how the little sheep loved to sit near the open fire.
The night sounds were precious;
The quiet, so peaceful and serene.

She began to thank the Shepherd.
"Thank You for always being so kind and understanding,
For looking after me in the pasture for such a long time,
And for the big sheep."

The Shepherd stopped her.
She was avoiding the issue.
"Little sheep, I know what's bothering you, but I want you to tell Me."
Miss Petite couldn't take it any longer.
She broke down in a flood of tears.
How often she had cried in front of the Shepherd.
What a big baby she was!
But He always seemed to understand
That tears were hurts from inside.

The Shepherd had a stern look on His face now.
"I insist you carry on with your story."
So she explained how she was in pain
And tired from walking from the flock to the pasture,
And climbing the hill to where the Shepherd usually stood.
She told him she was afraid to say anything
Should He think her ungrateful for all His care for her
When she was sick.
She was afraid of mocking and scorning sheep.
They would laugh and say that the Shepherd
Hadn't taken care of her at all,
Or that she was pretending to be sick to avoid the flock;
That they might criticize the Shepherd for not really healing her.

I Shall Not Want

The Shepherd had been such a comfort to her.

The Shepherd waited and watched the fire.
Miss Petite was silent.
She wasn't asking the Shepherd for anything more.
She was simply relating her story as the Shepherd had asked her to do.
The Shepherd moved the coals around in the fire.
"What is your real concern?" He asked, finally.

"Well," said the sheep cautiously.
"Will I ever be able to walk,
To run and jump with the flock?"
She had forgotten what it was like to run.

"Little sheep, would it be so terrible if you couldn't walk
With the other sheep?
Could you be content in a pasture
If you could visit the other sheep from time to time?
Have you ever looked at the sheep in the pasture
Who are never able to go back to the flock?
Have you noticed them sitting or lying there, some unable to move?
How many times are they visited by other sheep from the flock?
Have you spent all this time enjoying the pasture,
Never noticing other sheep around you
In the same predicament as you
And some even worse?
Little sheep, have you not noticed?"

I Shall Not Want

I Shall Not Want

Of course Miss Petite had noticed some,
But she had never really looked.
She was afraid to look.
She didn't want to be like them.
She didn't know what to say to them
Or how to act around them.
She had even chosen a special place in the pasture
Where she wouldn't have to look
At these other sheep lying around.
She couldn't bring herself to face any of them,
Not even the little lambs.
As long as she didn't have to acknowledge their presence,
She could pretend they didn't exist.

Miss Petite looked up at the Shepherd
Knowing how feeble her story sounded.
"I do want to run and jump and be like all the other sheep!
I'd tell them anything You want me to tell them.
Just as I told the big sheep about the bells,
I would tell any of the other sheep
Things that You want them to know.
I could go from sheep to sheep, up and down the flock.
I could run in and out of the flock
And carry messages all day long for You.
I could talk to the sheep
And You'd not have to use Your crook."

She could go on, but decided to stop.
The Shepherd wasn't really listening anyway.

The Shepherd began.
"And what about all the sheep in the pasture
Who don't have anyone to talk to?
What about those who are too weak to read
And those lambs who haven't yet learned to read?
If you find it so tiring to go up and down the pasture hill
And as it wears you out walking back and forth
To the flock,
Wouldn't it be wise to remain
In the pasture where the ground is level?

You could run freely in the pasture
Without other sheep bumping or tripping you.
And as you run, little sheep,
Could you not stop and talk to the other sheep in the pasture?"

The little sheep didn't even care now
If the Shepherd got cross with her.
"My dear Shepherd, it is too slow!" she whined.

"And what about Me?" the Shepherd said.
"Do you see Me running up and down the flock?
Do you see Me racing about?
No, little sheep, the sheep come to Me when I call them.
Sometimes they come because they want to talk to Me
Or because they need help or advice.
Don't be afraid, little one.
You will make lots of new friends amongst
The sheep lying up in the pasture.
You will also be able to call to the sheep of the flock
And they will come to you
Because you are exuberant.
You have something to share with them."

"Don't be afraid.
I will be with you
And I'll never leave you, little sheep."

Chapter 5

SORE LEGS

Miss Petite was lying next to the fire
In the still night.
The Shepherd stoked the fire and
Quietly tip-toed over to the little sheep,
And stroked her head.
He rubbed her back and legs.
The little sheep slipped into sleep.

The Shepherd stole away
To walk around the pasture to check the others,
And then returned to the little sheep.
He softly ran His fingers through her wool,
Separating the matted wool, gently removing burrs and ticks,
And then, He threw the grubs into the fire.
He was careful not to awaken her,
So she wouldn't know what had been removed from her wool.

The Shepherd sang softly.
Tears dropped from His eyes onto her small head.
He loved this sheep so.
She had become one of His very special ones.

She used to be so exuberant, lively and spirited.
She had been independent, self-sufficient
And sometimes arrogant.

I Shall Not Want

She had managed everything
And everyone had allowed her to do so.
Now, although she still spoke out of turn on occasion,
She was different;
More loving and caring.
She had learned those things from M. LeGrand,
The Shepherd reflected.
But more, her heart was right.

Quietly the Shepherd talked to Miss Petite as she slept,
Reminding her that He cared for her in many ways,
And knew her heart's desires.
He rubbed her legs with ointment to ease the pain.
He laid His hands on her back and His heart cried.
The Shepherd felt the depth of every hurt through His hands.
He wept;
Not because the sheep was maimed,
But because she did not fully trust Him yet,
Though she had spent
Hours and days, learning at the Shepherd's feet.
Perhaps she had spent too long with the big sheep,
Because he also did not trust the Shepherd.
It would be too heavy a load to try to explain
The complete plan to the little sheep,
The matter of trust would only confuse her.
No, it is best to wait for her to learn one day at a time.
Perhaps she is trying to walk on her own too soon.
She needs support from the big sheep.
She needs someone from the flock to tell her that I love her.
She is not listening to Me right now because she is so hurt.

Miss Petite awoke early
To the Shepherd leaning over her,
Caring for her.
Getting up was a struggle, so she drifted off to sleep.
The Shepherd whispered:
"You could have asked me to help you to your feet."
Not wanting to admit there was a problem,
And no longer feeling angry,
She accepted her plight,

I Shall Not Want

And chose to ignore the Shepherd's offer.

She opened one eye, just in time,
To catch a final tear
Dropping from the Shepherd's eye.
Concerned, she reassured the Shepherd
That she did love Him.
"I know, my little one, I know," He said, patting her head.

Throughout the day, the little sheep sat in the pasture
And thought about the conversation with the Shepherd
On the previous day.
She scanned the pasture slowly
Counting the number of sheep
Who were incapacitated in some way.
She lost count.
She couldn't begin to see them all!

"How could I have run, jumped and played without
Falling over some of them?" she puzzled.
Still she had managed to seclude herself
Without having to face the other sheep.
"Someday, I will become acquainted with them,
But not yet," she decided.
She was still learning to cope with her own pain.

"Why am I trying to act like it doesn't hurt anymore?
Who am I trying to impress?
I don't want anyone to criticize the Shepherd
For not healing me totally,
But I don't want them to criticize me
For not having the faith to receive it either.
I'm not ready for that!
I don't care whether they think I am a baby,
Or call me names."

And with that comment, into the unknown,
She moved off to a corner of pasture to be by herself,
Alone and quiet.

I Shall Not Want

Later in the day, the Shepherd came.
"Would you like to return to the flock
To visit M. LeGrand?"

She shook her head.
"No. He has so many things to think about.
He doesn't need me butting into his thoughts!"

"But he cares for you and needs to know
You are not angry with him.
Besides, he would walk slowly for you
And not embarrass you by mentioning your back legs.
You know that, little sheep.
He has never hurt you before.
In fact, he helped you many times
When you stumbled along the path with him," the Shepherd said.

"Sure enough," she thought, "the big sheep held me up
Those times when my legs gave out."

Vivid thoughts of a time when the pain was
Increasing in her legs and back, had caused her to panic.
She found every excuse to be near M. LeGrand,
And had made a nuisance of herself,
Tripping him; putting him off balance.
"No!" she thought. "I am going to have to learn
To take care of myself.
Besides, who says the pain isn't going to go away?
One of these days I will awaken perfectly whole
Because the Shepherd will have willed it for me.
The Shepherd loves me,
He will not allow me to go on like this.
It is only a test for me," she went on thinking to herself.
The little sheep was jolted back to reality by
The voice of the Shepherd.
"Oh, no! I do not want to disturb the big sheep.
I can manage just fine, I'm sure," she said.

"Perhaps you would like to write down all the things
That you have learned in the pasture," said the Shepherd.
"You could send them invitations
To join you for a short time in the pasture;
Or you could write the funny things you see happening
In the flock, from your vantage point.
You might even want to tell them about the sky."

"The sky?" the little sheep asked.
"The sky? I haven't even looked at the sky.
Why would I want to tell them about that!"

"The sheep in the flock walk with their heads down, eating.
Very few take time to look up.
It seems, my little sheep, you haven't either.
Take time, my little one and you shall learn much."

Miss Petite was humbled
And looked down to avoid the Shepherd's eyes.
But, in so doing, she noticed yet another burr in her wool.
She searched for the Shepherd's eyes now
And without speaking asked the Shepherd to remove the burr.

Chapter 6

PERMISSION

Day after day passed.
Miss Petite sat in the pasture.
She enjoyed her time here now
And did not want to return to the flock.
Occasionally she would offer a smile,
Or a greeting to the other sheep in the pasture.

Sheep from the flock had missed her,
And voluntarily came to visit.
Sometimes, one would leave as another came;
Sometimes, two arrived at once — not intentionally, of course.
The little sheep showed her visitors around the pasture,
If she felt there was an interest,
Or she would talk to them about the Shepherd.

She never discussed her pain and misery,
But instead listened to the accounts of their daily lives.
She wondered how they could stand such boring lives.
It seemed that the extent of their days was eating, sleeping and walking.

Although the little sheep often heard the others
Comment on her lifestyle of separation,
She never envied the other sheep.
She realized that no matter how much she talked
Of the quietness and peacefulness of the pasture,

And the goodness of the Shepherd,
These sheep would never understand
Unless they experienced it for themselves.

When she was alone,
She wrote, as the Shepherd had suggested.
She lay in the sun, looking at the sky.
"Why did the Shepherd suggest I gaze at the sky?
There is nothing there, no cloud, just blue sky!
Oh well, it is clear, beautiful and undisturbed."

Miss Petite was experiencing a new phase;
She was trembling and cold.
No matter how warm the sun, she was always cold.
Her legs were so shaky she could hardly write.

"Why did the Shepherd suggest I write?
No one could read my writing.
It looks like scribbles."

I Shall Not Want

"If I send these invitations to anyone,
They will throw them in the mud.
Any sheep would be insulted to receive
Such a poorly written message."
"Besides," the little sheep reflected,
"There have been so many sheep
Visiting that I don't really need
To send them invitations!"

But then, she thought,
"I could thank them for coming.
Yes. I will write them and tell them
How grateful I am that they left the flock
To spend time with me."

Before Miss Petite could get
Her pretty little cards together,
She was overcome by a miserable spell.
She lay in the pasture and moaned to herself.
She didn't want to call the Shepherd
For He was busy now with other sheep.
She didn't really need comfort anyhow.
It was simply a matter of enduring it.

She sang softly to herself
And watched the birds flit over her head.
She was not unhappy.
She was not even feeling sorry for herself.
She just knew the Shepherd loved her and
That He knew what she was going through.

After a time, another sheep from this pasture,
Whom she had once known from the flock,
Came over to her
And lay down beside her
And asked the little sheep to snuggle in close.
She was happy to see this sheep.
Many months ago, even when she was sick,
She had gone to help this sheep.
Miss Petite listened to the visitor talking

About how helpless he felt
And how discouraged he was with himself
That he wasn't up doing the things
He normally would be doing.

He wanted to believe like the little sheep
That the Shepherd loved him too,
But he was confused from listening
To other sheep in the flock.
He no longer knew right from wrong.
He had been persuaded that
If the Shepherd really did love him,
He would not have become sick.

Miss Petite recognized those words.
She remembered very well some of those
Same thoughts in her mind.
She turned to the visitor and asked if
He wanted to go to the Shepherd now.
"I will go with you. Once you have the opportunity
To speak directly to the Shepherd,
To meet Him personally,
You will understand and know inside
That the Shepherd does indeed love you."

The visitor paused and said, "Some day,
Some day I will, but not today.
I just want to lie here beside you.
It will give us both comfort."

Days passed,
And each new day brought something new and exciting.
One day, a strong sheep came from the flock to visit.
He didn't have trouble finding her; he had been there before.
"Come join me in the flock.
I realize you are still not feeling well,
But you could crawl up on my back!
From there you will be able to see so much!" he said excitedly.
"You can tell me what you are seeing,
And I promise, I will go very slowly for you."

I Shall Not Want

Miss Petite pondered the proposition,
And knew this sheep was gentle and strong
And would not get tired of carrying her.
She knew that he would also listen to her chatter,
Even if she talked too much.
She remembered how Forte, the strong sheep,
Liked to read books,
But now she could sit on his back and read to him.
He would like that, no doubt.
She could write her letters and cards while Forte moved slowly,
And would stop if it became too bumpy to write.
Forte liked exotic food
And was willing to venture
To areas along the path
That few sheep would use for gathering nourishment.
He would not take Miss Petite to the cliff side.

"Oh, I can't decide!" she thought to herself.
"It's all so exciting!
I would be with the flock, yet separate.
I could do all the things I want to do,
Except to run and play and jump.
I could trade those things for these."

She told Forte "Wait a minute!
I have to ask the Shepherd."
And off she trotted to see if the Shepherd had any objection.
She was surprised to see a long line
Of sheep waiting to see the Shepherd.
What would she do?
She couldn't expect the strong sheep to sit
In the pasture all day waiting for an answer.
"No," she thought. "If I can't see the Shepherd
And get a clear answer from Him today,
I will just have to say 'no' to Forte."

So, without waiting in line, Miss Petite returned,
Explaining what had happened
And that she would rather wait for a clear answer.
She could maybe second guess the Shepherd,
But she was unwilling to take the chance.

"I understand," the strong sheep said.
"I often talk to the Shepherd, too.
Do not feel pressured. I will be back another time.
I'll be glad to have you join me anytime."

Chapter 7

DISAPPOINTMENT

Miss Petite meandered over to the Shepherd,
Plopped herself full length beside Him,
Rolled over on her back,
Crossed her leg one over the other
And folded her front legs behind her head.
Her eyes told the Shepherd that she didn't really want
Conversation or questions.
She just didn't want to be alone.
Every once in a while,
A tear trickled down her face.

The Shepherd did not intrude in her thoughts.
He stood, quietly.
Then He began to hum.
"Please don't hum.
It reminds me of the big sheep!" she said.

She jumped up as quickly as she had lain down.
The Shepherd stepped backwards and
Looked at Miss Petite.
"How did you manage to jump up
From the position you were in;
From lying on your back?" the Shepherd asked.

I Shall Not Want

"Ha! Ha! I made sure I lay on Your staff.
That way, I could roll a bit and it was just enough
To push me right over!"

The Shepherd picked up His staff
Which He had left on the ground earlier,
And was amazed
At how much Miss Petite had learned
During her time in the pasture.

"Do you want to talk about it?" the Shepherd asked.
"Well," the little sheep said,
"A number of sheep are asking me
To do things with them;
To walk with them and eat with them."
"So, why does that upset you?" queried the Shepherd.

"Well, these sheep are good sheep.
They like You and listen to You,
But they aren't M. LeGrand."

"Would they harm you?" the Shepherd asked.

"No, not really.
Some might, and I would ask You first,
If I had any doubt about anything.
Others would be very good to me
And would see that no harm came to me;
They would take me places
And would share exciting things with me."

"So?" the Shepherd raised His eyebrows, waiting.

"Well, there is one who is being very kind
And has offered to stay close beside me,
But he is doing it to be malicious," she said quietly.

"Can you not stay away from that particular sheep?" He said.

"Yes, but he always seems to find me,
Even when I stay with a bigger sheep."

"Why are you afraid
Of hurting M. LeGrand, my little one?" He asked.

"The big sheep doesn't want me so close.
I can't blame him, my dear Shepherd.
I was becoming such a nuisance,
Because I was so lonely.
I was walking too close to him
And found my feet under his hooves.
Oh, he was so careful not to step on me,
But I kept throwing him off balance
And when I stuck my head under his to get his attention,
He could neither walk nor eat.
My dear Shepherd, I do miss the big sheep so very much,
But I cannot go back to him.
I have caused such problems for him."

The Shepherd, as usual, had listened
And knew it wasn't the other sheep
Upsetting Miss Petite.
It was that she couldn't deal with
Her feelings for M. LeGrand.

I Shall Not Want

I Shall Not Want

She continued.
"I want the big sheep to get all combed out,
To get the bugs out of his wool.
I want him to have the most beautiful set of bells.
I want him to play on the knoll;
That all these sheep and sheep of other flocks
Would hear his music.
I want the big sheep to be happy with himself
And with his music,
And with me."

The Shepherd knelt down beside Miss Petite
And began to pick the thistles from her wool.
He brushed the matted areas
And washed her front legs.
Meanwhile, she chattered on about her concerns and hurts
And her great wishes for M. LeGrand.

Suddenly, she realized what the Shepherd was doing,
And looked down at the pile of grubs
That the Shepherd had taken out of her wool.
She started to cry.
This couldn't have come from her.
She had prided herself in being so clean!
After all, she had stayed close to the Shepherd
To avoid getting those things on herself.

He started to explain that as long as
She was part of the flock
And associating with other sheep,
She would be bumping up against them
And her wool would naturally pick up
Some of the briars, burrs, thistles or ticks.
Then He said, "And your muddy front legs;
Were you off the path, my little one?"

Shamefaced, the little sheep looked up at the Shepherd;
"I went to the edge of the cliff with another sheep
And looked over.
There was mud there, but my dear Shepherd,
You can see I didn't go over,
Because my back legs are not dirty."

"So I noticed, little one.
But must you go so close to the edge?"

The Shepherd began to explain the dangers that might be ahead.
"Your wool is thicker and longer now;
You may pick up things more easily.
Because you look bigger and stronger
And the big sheep is no longer taking care of you,
Some sheep might expect more from you.
Some might push and shove;
Some might innocently believe you want company
And want to walk with them.
Some sheep might deliberately take advantage of you.
So now, little sheep, you must be much more careful.
You cannot depend on M. LeGrand to protect you,
Or defend you; you cannot go running to him
Every time you want his help."

"But," the little sheep cut in.
"I didn't go to him just for protection
And to get him to fight my battles for me.
I went to him to share things.
I told him everything!"

The Shepherd looked at her,
With His penetrating gaze.
"I understand, little sheep,
But did he?"

I Shall Not Want

Miss Petite was suddenly very sad inside.
She liked M. Le Grand so much.
She had no interest in walking beside any other sheep.
Even while standing beside the Shepherd,
She could look out over the entire flock
And see not even one sheep she'd like to walk beside.

Miss Petite asked the Shepherd
If He could just stay beside her for awhile.
She didn't want to have to fend for herself
And she didn't want to return to M. LeGrand.

The Shepherd had no objections
And asked if they could sing together.
The little sheep smiled and jumped into the Shepherd's arms,
And the two of them sang heartily together.
The little sheep even tried to teach Him
The one chorus M. LeGrand had taught her;
"I've been changed!"

Chapter 8

THE SHELTER

Although Miss Petite loved visitors,
And thoroughly enjoyed having the sheep
From the flock come to visit,
She was a little tired from it all.
She was thankful for the many diversions
Over the past several days.
None of the other sheep could possibly know
That she needed other things to think about.
She enjoyed the visit
From one sheep in the pasture
Who couldn't possibly have known of her hurts.
She had told no one except the Shepherd.

The little sheep decided it was time to rest.
No more visitors today, she thought.
How could she not welcome another sheep
If one came by to see her?
She got up and marked off a square with her hooves.
It was a big enough square to sit inside
And not be cramped.
At least she wasn't greedy in taking up
Too much pasture.

I Shall Not Want

Just then, the Shepherd, who was walking through the pasture
Checking on the sheep who were weak or ill,
Came to her and asked what she was doing.
She explained she wanted time alone
And was marking off a square for herself.
No one would cross that line.
She needed privacy and a chance to be quiet.
She didn't want to be brooding about anything,
Just some time to be alone.

"Would it help if I build you a shelter of your own?" the Shepherd asked.

"A shelter for me?" the little sheep asked.
"Oh dear Shepherd, would you do that for me?"

"Is that the size you want, little sheep?" He asked.
"It is quite modest. It could be made larger if you wish."
So the little sheep let the Shepherd build a place for her.
She helped the Shepherd
By holding boards and handing Him the nails,
And a saw, when necessary.

I Shall Not Want

This was another new adventure.
She had never helped the Shepherd build anything before.
What fun!
Miss Petite was awestruck by the construction.
She had only imagined a few boards around the side
For privacy,
The Shepherd began with a floor, a solid base.
From there the Shepherd put up walls,
Higher than the little sheep had dreamed of,
With windows cut into the walls to allow in the light.
The Shepherd even made a second floor,
With a ramp with little bars on it
So the little sheep could pull herself up
On those days she had difficulty walking.
The upstairs was like a tower,
A vantage point to view the pasture
And flocks in every direction.

She couldn't believe it.
She would have been content with a line
Drawn to mark her own corner,
But the Shepherd offered a shelter.
Four walls would have been enough,
But this was beyond her imagination.
It was a roof over her head,
But more, a tower to see the world.

Overwhelmed, she could not find the words
To thank the Shepherd.
The Shepherd knew words were not enough,
And waved to the little sheep as He went on His way.
Miss Petite paced from side to side in the tower,
Soaking in the view.
She could hear some sheep bleating from the other flocks
When the wind blew from a certain direction.
"Were they bleating for help?" she asked herself.

A long time passed before the little sheep
Returned to the bottom floor.
The Shepherd had put a rug in the shelter.

It was too beautiful to sleep on.
Perhaps she could use it to cover herself in the cold.
She decided to tack the rug to the outside wall
So she could share it with the other sheep.
One by one, the sheep came to admire the shelter and the rug.
Some were genuinely happy and congratulated her.

Most were jealous.
Some told her she was spoiled
And must have thrown a tantrum for the Shepherd to do this.
Some told her she wasn't very considerate of the other sheep
In the pasture.
They had to sleep in the sunshine and the rain.
"Some sheep are in worse condition than you," they said.

Miss Petite was broken-hearted.
She thought everyone would like her shelter
And think the Shepherd wonderful for His provision.
She pretended the remarks meant nothing
And tried to explain that the Shepherd had started
With a firm base, that it hadn't been difficult to build
And had taken no time at all.

When everyone left, she curled up in a corner.
Was she being selfish?
What about all the other sick sheep in the pasture?
That wasn't her worry.
Those sheep could have shelters too, if they wanted;
They only had to ask the Shepherd.
She would enjoy the shelter and no one would take away her pleasure.

"Where was Miss Bow, the lady with the pink ribbon by her ear?"
She thought to herself,
"She comes by quite regularly to see me and help me walk."
She had become such a friend and she loved the Shepherd, too.
They walked and talked about their love for the Shepherd and
His love for them.
Miss Bow was wise and gracious and taught her many things,
In gentle ways that did not offend.
"Maybe she will come tomorrow.

She would know that I have had too many visitors today.
She will love it!"

She changed the rug to another wall of the shelter
That faced the pasture, for more sheep to enjoy.
One sheep called out, "What are you doing, little sheep,
Trying to rub it in that you have a shelter?"
Miss Petite was devastated.
She took the hanging down and put it on a wall on the inside.

There was a knock at the door entrance.
Surprised, she turned to see the old sheep
She had befriended a few years ago.
They had parted company, but now, here he was.
The little sheep invited her old friend in.
It was the hospitable thing to do.
The friend sat quiet for a long time, and
Then congratulated her on the shelter.
He went on to say she deserved it,
And that he should know, because he knew her very well.
Confused, the little sheep accepted the comments from the heart
Refusing to believe that this was intended to be malicious.
He gave a couple of suggestions; improvements that could be made;
Helpful hints, and as he was leaving, said,
"By the way, I've already built a ramp
Up to a treehouse over yonder."
The little sheep knew now why the old friend had come.
She laughed out loud when the friend got out of sight and earshot.
She knew that even if the friend had built a ramp to the sky,
It could not be the same as hers because
He had not asked the Shepherd for help.

She sat down to relax.
All the visitors had come and gone.
It was getting late and she was tired.
But now, what was this she was seeing?
"Oh well, one never knows,
Some day, an angel might come knocking at the door."
The little sheep went out to greet her latest visitors.
They were elderly sheep and had been together for years.

I Shall Not Want

They knew the Shepherd quite well.
She invited them in and they looked over the shelter
With one eye between them.
"What do you think you're doing, little sheep?
Why are you creating more problems for yourself?
The Shepherd told you to rest, and here you go
Building a shelter with a ramp, no less.
You're just going to wear yourself out
And not be any good for anything," the elderly lady sheep said.

She should have expected this blow,
But always hoped these two sheep
Would some day be more pleasant.
She tried to explain that it was the Shepherd's idea;
That He had built this beautiful shelter for her.
The elderly male sheep broke in;
"I don't believe you.
The Shepherd would never have built this for you.
You are not well enough to use this shelter.
You shouldn't even be alone yet.
Don't tell me the Shepherd did it for you. You did it yourself!"
Miss Petite realized it had been a long time since
These two sheep had listened to her.
She wanted to tell them how she danced around happily
Because the Shepherd let her go free.
She wanted to defend the Shepherd,
To explain how the shelter came to be.

But the lady sheep cut in again sharply with her questions;
"And what about M. LeGrand?
Why isn't he here to give you a hand?
And look at you! You're still not walking straight!
Did he run away when he realized you'd never walk properly again?
Oh, it's all right when you're strong and capable!
He can lean on you then.
But what about now, little sheep,
Can he not bear it now?"

I Shall Not Want

The accusations against M. LeGrand were cutting,
But she felt almost guilty, because it had been some time now
Since she had thought of the big sheep.
She took her time answering the questions
They had finished speaking, and waited.
Initially, she wanted to tell them to leave, and
Not come back.
But she remembered someone teaching her
That she must never needlessly burn bridges.
Boards can be repaired, but bridges cannot.

She took a deep breath, and told the couple
Politely and calmly that the Shepherd had indeed
Built the shelter, and she was very happy with it.
She was trusting the Shepherd for healing.
As for M. LeGrand, it was none of their business.
He had always been considerate and helpful to her,
And it was unfair to accuse him so.
She asked that they would never do that again.

The elderly lady sheep made one last comment in her defense.
"Well, little sheep, I don't care what you do with M. LeGrand;
We certainly won't interfere!"
They left, but the little sheep did not initiate a return visit.
A sudden calm settled on her as she went back into the house.
Where had that come from?

The sun was setting and the night air was chilly.
Miss Petite thought about the open fire.
She would not be sleeping by it tonight.
She would miss that, and the music.
Just as she was dozing off, she heard
The Shepherd outside her door.
Just a short distance away,
The Shepherd was building a fire pit for the little sheep.
He started the fire and stoked it up with lots of wood for the night.
She could not believe what she was seeing.
The Shepherd had given her this beautiful shelter,
But He had not taken anything away.

I Shall Not Want

Miss Petite thanked the Shepherd again and again,
Knowing that it would never be enough.
The Shepherd expected nothing more than the expression of thanks.
He came over and patted her head,
And told her He would be back to put ointment on her legs.
Ointment? She had never known that He had done this before.
He must have done it while she was sleeping.

It was too much to take in. She just wanted to sleep.
She heard the Shepherd humming off in the distance,
As He tended to the other sheep.
"I've been changed."
She curled up tightly and went to sleep.

Chapter 9

CRIES OF THE WORLD

On awakening in the morning,
The first thing the little sheep did
Was climb to the upper level.
Though difficult, she did it without complaining.
She wanted to look out at the foreign flocks.
What bleating! There must be lots of sheep calling.
Why were they calling? What could be their trouble?
The sheep in her own flock weren't bleating like that.
She couldn't stand the sound in her ears.
Something dreadful must be wrong.
She wondered if the Shepherd had not heard the bleating.

She rushed over to the Shepherd,
(Forgetting to be thankful for the shelter and the peaceful sleep),
And blurted out, "Why are those sheep bleating?
It's terrible! Why isn't something done to help them?
They must need help!"

The Shepherd said they did that all the time.
"What made you hear them all of a sudden?"

The little sheep explained that she had gone
To the upper level of her shelter both evening and morning,
And heard the bleating cries of the foreign flocks.
"It is so sad, and I can't stand the crying.
What is wrong with them?" said the little sheep.

"It is time for me to walk through the pasture
To check on the sickly and the weak," the Shepherd said.
Seeking an answer to her question, the little sheep
Tagged along with the Shepherd on His morning check.
"I check the foreign flocks just like my own,
But some of the bigger sheep in their flocks
Have not allowed the other sheep to come to me,
Even if they desire to do so."

"Well, can't you make the bigger sheep step aside?"
the little sheep asked.

"Oh yes, little sheep, I can make them,
But as I have explained to you over and over again,
I do not wish to make any sheep do anything
He does not wish to do on his own.
I'd much rather the bigger sheep decide themselves
That the little sheep can come to me
And themselves as well, for that matter."
"What about the others, are they all the same?" the little sheep continued.

"No," the Shepherd said.
"Some sheep are just constant complainers.
No matter what I do for them they complain.
Others have refused to let Me help them
And have ended up in trouble.
Still others don't want My help even when their troubles are many.
Some have gone off the path
And have indigestion from eating the wrong type of food.
Little sheep, there is no end to the cries out there
But I can only do for them what they will let Me do."

Miss Petite couldn't understand why a sheep wouldn't
Let the Shepherd do things for him.
The whole time they walked and talked,
The Shepherd stopped to speak to each sheep in the pasture.
She had not really seen any of them at all.
She had walked by them.
"Walked by them?" she gasped.
"I was with the Shepherd, and I walked by them
And never said so much as 'good morning.'
How could I have done such a thing!
Well, I will just have to go around and apologize to each one," she said to herself.

So, she started out by speaking to each sheep
That she had intentionally snubbed.
Sometimes she'd ask them how they were or
Whether she could get them something.
Sometimes she would get a cold cloth for a headache
Or a cup of cold water.
Sometimes she'd just sing a song.
Miss Petite was amazed at the number of sheep lying there
Who had never actually talked to the Shepherd
As He passed by every day.
Before too long, Miss Petite found herself
At the end of the pasture,
Having met all the sheep she had missed in the morning.
There, standing in front of her, was the Shepherd Himself.

"Oh" the little sheep said, "I've met a whole lot of sick sheep
In the pasture this morning.
Some require a lot of attention."
She talked to the Shepherd about all those sheep she hadn't seen
Because she hadn't stayed with the Shepherd for the complete round.
The Shepherd said there would be time enough to meet them all,
But was delighted she had gone on her own to meet the sheep where they were.

I Shall Not Want

Chapter 10

THE BOOK

Miss Petite reviewed the lessons
The Shepherd had taught her so long ago.
She had kept good notes
And that was a bonus now
Because her legs had become wobbly
And her script scribbly.

The Shepherd had given her a book to read as well.
She wondered if it was the same book
That the Shepherd had given to M. LeGrand.
She began to read it and was so fascinated
That she couldn't put it down.
Before the Shepherd began to teach her,
She had started by reading a verse or two;
Then, she was reading chapters at a time.
Now, again, she was eating up the book!
She hadn't noticed too many other sheep reading it.
Maybe they didn't have this book.
She wondered whether M. LeGrand had this book,
And whether he was as fascinated with it as she was.

She knew that Miss Bow
Must have this book,
Because she had talked of it often,
And they had repeated the same words
To each other when they talked together.

"How can it be the same book
If we don't all have the same questions?" she asked herself.
"Oh well, it is just one more thing I will have to ask the Shepherd.
I'd better make a list."
And with that, she looked up to see who was there.

The Shepherd had been standing there waiting
For Miss Petite to ask Him those questions.
"Little sheep, would you like to go for a walk with Me,
Or would you rather stay here and talk?" He asked.

"Well, perhaps we could stay here today.
When I have questions, I can refer to my book
And You can help me understand.
Would You mind, Dear Shepherd?"
"That will be fine, little one. Where shall we begin?
What would you like to know first?"
The little sheep thought for a moment.
She had so many things to ask
And some were more important that others.
She didn't want to sound overanxious or ungrateful,
So she weighed in her mind which subject to approach first.

Suddenly, she blurted out,
"Dear Shepherd, what is the greatest
Secret of all in life?"
Just as quickly as it was asked,
The Shepherd replied, "Love."

Both were silent.
"Love. How could that be?" thought the little sheep.
Miss Petite didn't know much about love.
She guessed she loved M. LeGrand.
That was probably as close as she had come
To really loving someone.

She thought of different sheep she knew;
Miss Bow, the sheep with the pink ribbon;
Forte, the strong sheep who offered her a ride on his back;
So many sheep that she really didn't love,
Or want to.
She didn't even really like the sheep in the pasture
And they were her neighbors.
At least she was getting to know them better.

Thoughts of love and what it might be
Whirled around in Miss Petite's head,
Until she came back to reality and gasped,
"Oh! My Dear Shepherd, You loved me long ago
And now I have learned to love You!"

"That is right, my little one.
Once you learned to love Me,
You began to love the other sheep too," He said.

"Oh no, my Dear Shepherd.
I don't love the other sheep.
Maybe some of them, but not many!"

"That will come with time, little sheep.
You don't wish them bad things, do you?"

"Of course not, Dear Shepherd.
In fact, even those sheep I don't like very well,
I wish only good."
"By hoping they see good and receive good,
They too might become good."

"See?" the Shepherd said. "That is a form of love.
Don't let anyone take that from you."

"Dear Shepherd, Miss Bow,
And Promise, who read the book,
Have taught me much about love,
If that is what You call love."

"Yes, little sheep, that is correct,
For they have both learned from me.
They have been faithful students
And remembered their lessons well."

Miss Petite was still thinking of M. LeGrand.
"He taught me about love too," she thought.
"Would the Shepherd be insulted if
I raised the subject with Him?"

"Little sheep, the big sheep has taught you about love too,
And you must not forget that," said the Shepherd.
She wondered how He knew her thoughts.
He continued.
"M. Le Grand showed you a caring love.
Look, little sheep,
The two lady sheep gave of their time in love;
And so did the big sheep.
But even more than that,
M. Le Grand carried you in his heart.
Oh, he told you many things;
That you were too small, for instance.
Remember how you were so little
You could crawl right under him,
To walk to the other side?"

They both laughed.

He wanted to make sure she would hear Him,
And it seemed the little sheep was allowing herself
To be hurt all over again.
He waited until she was following Him again.
"My little one,
Love starts in the heart, not in the mind."

How could the Shepherd in those few moments
Have given her so much to ponder?
All those questions she had to ask
Were now unimportant.
Her questions were all about love, now.
So many questions to ask Him about love.

The Shepherd stood and said He had to go.
He'd be back to talk another time about love.
He suggested the little sheep read in His little book,
"Make love your great quest."
The little sheep sat open-mouthed staring at the Shepherd.
She didn't even think to write down what He told her.
The Shepherd knew she would find the verses herself,
When she opened the book.

Something nibbled at the corner of her brain.
"I know there was something I forgot to ask Him," she thought.
She stretched in the sun for awhile,
And looked up at the sky.
The sky; the sounds in the pasture;
The smell of the grass; the stillness of the air;
Something.

She flipped through the book
As she lay in the grass looking up at the sky,
Looking at the words, but not really seeing.
"The Lord is my Shepherd." (2)
Funny, she had never seen that before.
"The Lord is my Shepherd", she realized;
"But my Shepherd is here" — she began to sputter.
"That must mean my Shepherd is the LORD!
My, oh my, I have never thought of that before!"

I Shall Not Want

She decided she'd have to find the Shepherd right away
And ask Him if that was true.
She looked around and sure enough,
The Shepherd was only a few feet away.
She was amazed at how close He was,
Just when she needed Him.

She hurried over to Him,
And her tongue got as tangled as her feet.
"My dear Lord, I mean, My Dear Shepherd, or should I say Lord?"
The Shepherd grinned and leaned down
To steady the little sheep.
"My Dear Shepherd, I was reading in the book You gave me
'The Lord is my Shepherd'. Is that right? Are You the Lord?"

The Shepherd crouched down by the little sheep
And whispered in her ear.
"Little sheep, I am the good Shepherd;
Have I not called you and all the other sheep by name?
Have I not bathed your wounds,
Healed your sick hearts,
And guided you along the path?
Have I not made provisions for you as necessary?
Little sheep, do I not love you?"

Miss Petite was so humbled,
She could not look at the Shepherd.
She bowed her head as though to worship,
Although she had no idea what worship meant.
The Shepherd asked her if she had read the whole Psalm.
"Oh, no, dear Shepherd, when I read the first line,
I just had to come to see You!"

"Bless you, little sheep," He said.
"You are so impulsive, but I love that about you.
Go, and read the rest of the words."
Miss Petite stood and walked away muttering under her breath; 'Bless you.'
"What did the shepherd, my Lord, mean by 'bless you'?"

2. Psalm 23:1, <u>Spirit Filled Life Bible</u>, **NKJV**, Thomas Nelson Publishers, Nashville, TN., USA, 1991.

Chapter 11

A HEALING, A SONG AND A HEART'S DESIRE

Miss Petite had been visited by many sheep
Who took no thought
Of her feelings, her welfare, or activities.
They never asked if it was convenient for her to sit in her shelter for a visit.
They just did.
It wasn't always a good time for Miss Petite
To entertain them,
But she graciously set things aside
And made room and time for her guests.

It was days like this, when her health was poor;
When she was tired and worn, completely drained;
When she couldn't remember whether it had been a dream or reality;
But it was about a shepherd.
It was not her Shepherd who had now become her Lord,
But about a shepherd who was mean.
The little sheep was grateful that it had only been a dream,
And thanked her Shepherd under her breath.
But she couldn't sleep, and lay restless and feverish for hours.

All morning, she could not function.
Visitors came and went;
She hadn't offered them tea or soup,
And their idle chit-chat
Made her feel even worse than before.
She couldn't eat or drink;
She crawled into a corner in her shelter;
The flies buzzed around her head,
Her hips and back ached and she tossed and rolled in misery.

Miss Petite noticed the Shepherd peeking through the window.
Catching that glimpse of Him,
She asked if He could keep the flies away
And keep the noise down in the pasture.
She was desperately in need of peaceful rest.
The Shepherd assured her that He would
And in the blink of an eye the little sheep fell asleep.
She slept for hours and when she awoke
The silence of the pasture was unnerving.
She called out to thank the Shepherd.

I Shall Not Want

She didn't feel strong, but was rested,
And resigned to her lack of appetite.
Her legs and back felt much better;
In fact, so much so that there wasn't any pain.
Not anywhere.
She wasn't even gritting her teeth.
Why, she felt like she was ten feet tall!

Miss Petite wanted something special today from the Shepherd.
She asked the Shepherd if He would surprise her tonight
By showing her, or telling her something unique, just for her.
The Shepherd told her He would, but later.
The little sheep was disappointed, impatient.
She wondered if she had finally been too much of a nuisance.
Perhaps the Shepherd had no time for her anymore.
"Pull yourself together and behave like an adult,"
She said to herself.
"The Shepherd will come by when He is ready."

Darkness had settled in,
The stars shone,
But the Shepherd had not come.
She wasn't worried though.
The Shepherd had never broken a promise!

As she was pondering sheep concerns
Sniffing the breeze in the beautiful night,
She thought of the cries she heard now
That she had never heard before she had a shelter.
"I guess my moaning and groaning drowned them out!"
She chuckled to herself.
Suddenly she felt a gentle touch on her hips.
She turned, and there was the Shepherd.
How had He come up the ramp so quietly?
How long had He been sitting beside her, reading her thoughts?
It didn't matter.
Miss Petite was glad to know He was there beside her.

I Shall Not Want

"What special thing did you want this night?" queried the Shepherd.
"It doesn't matter now. I am just so happy to have You
Here beside me," she sighed.
The two remained silent for a long time.
Weariness still draped over the little sheep like a curtain,
So the Shepherd didn't expect much conversation tonight.

Miss Petite smiled and cried all at the same time,
And the Shepherd brushed away the tears.
He didn't have to ask why.
He knew she was overcome with joy
That she could run and jump,
And at the same time,
Sadness, that she could not share it with M. LeGrand.
She wanted to ask if this was only a temporary remission,
But decided this was not the night to ask.
"No pain, no sorrow. I must be happy.
Help me to be happy!" she thought to herself.

The Shepherd picked up the little sheep
And held her close.
Miss Petite was surprised.
She hadn't asked or expected such love
From the Shepherd.
Surely He must be tired Himself;
Surely there must be other sheep
Who would be looking for Him now, she thought.
The Shepherd laid His hand on her head and sang:
"The Lord bless you and keep you;
The Lord make His face shine upon you,
And be gracious to you;
The Lord lift up His countenance upon you,
And give you peace." (3)

The small one relaxed until her body was limp.
The Shepherd sang and she dozed.
Then He spoke gently to her;
"Little sheep, I love you.
You are impulsive and excitable.
Sometimes you rush in too quickly,

I Shall Not Want

But your heart is right and I love you for that.
Protect what I have given you.
Share, but do not throw away those precious gems of truth.
Study my book.
You don't understand the cry of the sheep but you will someday.
Have no fear my little one.
You are getting bigger now, and you can help the tiny sheep in the flock.
Prepare lessons for them. Write down the things I have taught you.
What you have forgotten, I will bring to your remembrance.
I love you little sheep. I will not leave you comfortless.
I will never forsake you, and
I will give you the desires of your heart."

Miss Petite was so relaxed and peaceful
She couldn't bring herself to say anything.
Drifting off, she heard Him say
That He would give her the desires of her heart,
But she could not think
Of what those desires would be.

Morning came and Miss Petite awoke
With healing in her bones and in her spirit.
She was jubilant in her heart.
She tidied up her shelter,
And decided to share her jubilation with the flock.
She barely spoke with the Shepherd,
Or stopped to read His book,
But skipped off to the flock as fast as she could.

She surprised the others by being there.
Some commented on how healthy she appeared,
How she seemed to be her old self.
Some laughed when she said
She couldn't stay in the flock;
How she hadn't been released from the pasture yet,
But was allowed to run and play with them only for a time.
One lady sheep called her lazy.
Many were not interested in what the Shepherd had taught her,
But wanted to know when she could eat and walk like them.
Some said she was spoiled and too dependent on the Shepherd.

She hadn't seen the big sheep.
The rude and thoughtless comments made her head hang low.
She returned to her shelter to pull herself together,
And though she saw the Shepherd in the distance,
She hoped that He would not come early.

The book the Shepherd had given her
Was lying in the middle of the floor.
Ashamed that she had found it in a heap,
Abused it somehow,
She picked it up, flipped through it,
And tried to remember the verse
The Shepherd had quoted to her the night before.
He did not say them but sang them to her.
"I must try that sometime, sing the words
From the book," she said.

I Shall Not Want

"The big sheep could put some music to these words.
He loves music and knows much more about music than I do.
I'll ask the Shepherd which words to take to him
That he might put it to music,"
And off she went to find the Shepherd.

She sought the Shepherd out
As He made His rounds in the pasture,
Amongst the sick and afflicted.
She also stopped and talked to some of them for a time.
When she asked the Shepherd about the words,
Without hesitation He already knew her desires,
And picked a verse He knew would suit her needs the best.
She was to read it in her shelter first, and she would understand
Why He had chosen those words.

She hurried back and grabbed her book,
Flipping through until she found the passage,
And read it carefully:
"These things have I spoken to you,
That in Me you may have peace.
In the world you will have tribulation;
But be of good cheer,
I have overcome the world." (4)

His words came back to Miss Petite
From the conversation of the evening before:
". . . Little sheep, you are getting bigger now,
And can help some of the tiny sheep in the flock.
You don't have to tangle with the bigger sheep. . .
Concentrate on the tiny sheep . . .
They need to learn . . .
Prepare lessons . . .
Write down what I have taught you . . ."

She tucked her book away and ran off to the flock
To find the big sheep.
She hadn't seen him for such a long time
And anticipated their reunion.

I Shall Not Want

Without any hesitation,
She rushed up to M. LeGrand
And snuggled in close to him to walk beside him.
The big sheep didn't seem pleased at all,
So rather than getting her feelings hurt all over again,
Miss Petite talked as fast as she could about the Shepherd
And the words from the book, and the music
That the big sheep could put to the words, if he would.
Miss Petite didn't go into detail about
What the Shepherd had been teaching her,
Or the bleating of the sheep in other flocks,
Or even about the tiny sheep.
M. LeGrand didn't answer,
Didn't nod his head,
Nor even recognize that she was there.
He certainly showed no interest in the little sheep's request.
She turned sadly to leave.
The big sheep called out:
"Little sheep, I am working on something,
But thanks for coming."

Oh, she wanted to go back and talk to him,
But she didn't dare.
She didn't want to get hurt again by his indifference.
She couldn't afford to go through turmoil again,
Not right now.

"I am able to walk, and run, and jump;
And the big sheep didn't even notice I could do these things.
Besides the Shepherd told me not to tangle
With the bigger sheep in the flock,
And I guess that means him, too."
She was resigned to the fact that the big sheep
Must have been glad for something, whatever that was,
And at least he thanked her for coming.

Miss Petite sat up by the open fire
And wrote into the night,
Continuing each day

Except for times when visitors stopped in.
She was thrilled that the Shepherd
Had given her something to do to fill her time.

She was diligent with her task.
Many days passed and she was beginning to
Get tired and irritable.
When visitors came, she found it hard
To contain her feelings and be hospitable.
Even when she wasn't feeling well,
She found it difficult to send visiting sheep away.
She didn't want to insult a friendly soul,
Even if sometimes they came out of curiosity.

One sheep came to edit,
One sheep came to read and discuss
And another with tiny sheep came to visit and understand.
She knew that they all came
To learn with her,
The lessons from the Shepherd.
Those were all who read her writings.

When Miss Petite was sick in the pasture,
She used to write down all the things happening
To her on scraps of paper,
And send them to M. LeGrand,
Via sheep express.
When he saw her he would say how much
He enjoyed getting her note,
And never criticized her for anything she said.
Many times they were words of misery;
Disgruntled over the pain, or of having to stay in the pasture.
Many times she repeated herself,
But sometimes she shared about the Shepherd
And His love.
M. LeGrand had hidden all those notes
Under a big rock, never losing one.
She wondered now, if the big sheep
Would even be interested to read some of the lessons

I Shall Not Want

She was working on.
She didn't want a confrontation, or to be snubbed altogether.

After pondering for some time,
She sat down and wrote a note to M. LeGrand,
Explaining the lessons she would be sending to him,
For his review.
If he didn't want them, he could return them.
"What if he thinks I mean these to be lessons for him?"
She said this to the Shepherd, who just happened to be passing by.

"Little sheep, where is your heart?"

Miss Petite knew what the Shepherd meant.
It wasn't a matter of where her heart was, but
Whether her heart was right, that really mattered.

So with new determination,
She packed up the lessons with a letter of explanation.
No matter that the big sheep ever spoke to her again.
Her heart was right, she was sure.
She would not be discouraged if no words came from M. LeGrand.
She was doing what the Shepherd had asked,
And that was all that mattered.

In the evening, after sending off the lesson to M. LeGrand,
Miss Petite thought about the Shepherd's promise:
"Little sheep, I will give you the desires of your heart."
She thought back to when she was a tiny sheep.
She wanted then to be big and strong.
That would have been her heart's desire then.
She recollected how she had wanted to become important, even famous.
That would have been her heart's desire as a youth.
She had had many ambitions and worked hard to achieve them.
Some went well, some failed.

She wasn't greedy, but her heart's desire then
Would have been to enjoy life
Without having to perpetually munch and walk.
Again she was confused.

"I wanted the big sheep to have all those bells,
To have his wool brushed out,
And yes, to walk beside him all the time."
She remembered talking to the Shepherd about those things.
That surely had been her heart's desire, not long ago.
Was that still her heart's desire?
She thought not.
How could she desire something that the big sheep
Definitely did not want?
There was no contact.
M. LeGrand had never come to visit,
Or to see the shelter,
Or comment on the lessons,
Or sent a note via sheep express.
Nothing.

Was she hurt?
She chose not to be.
She knew in her heart that her desire had changed.
She looked across the pasture at the Shepherd and smiled,
Warm and content.
"The only heart's desire I have now,
Is to do what the Shepherd wants me to do."

3. Numbers 6:24-26, <u>Spirit Filled Life Bible</u>, **NKJV**, Thomas Nelson Inc., Nashville, TN., USA, 1991.
4. Ibid., John 16:33.

Chapter 12

OBEDIENCE

Curled up in the corner alone,
Minutes passed like hours.
Miss Petite didn't like feeling this way.
It was a beautiful day
But she had no energy to put into it.
She would go out in the sunshine,
But she could not make herself get up.
She thought of the Shepherd, but said nothing.

The Shepherd slipped in quietly
And touched Miss Petite on the forehead.
He told her He understood why
She was unhappy inside.
"Do you want me to fetch the big sheep for you?
I will talk to him for you, or I could use the crook
Around his neck to bring him here to you,
If that is what you want," said the Shepherd.

She had resigned herself to not seeing him again.
The Shepherd didn't argue with Miss Petite.
He would have wiped her tears away,
But she refused to cry.
She asked Him to rub her heart
Because it seemed like it was cracking,
It hurt so much.

"Did you do any lessons today, little sheep?
Are you up for just one short lesson now?" the Shepherd said.
Miss Petite thought about it for a moment
And decided if the Shepherd was going to take time to teach it
Then she could take the time to learn from Him.

They opened the book together:
"Whoever therefore breaks one of the least of these
Commandments, and teaches men so,
Shall be called least in the kingdom of heaven;
But whoever does and teaches them,
He shall be called great in the kingdom of heaven." (5)

"Again, whoever disregards the least significant of the commands
I have given and teaches others to disregard them,
That sheep will become the least significant in my sheepfold;
But, whoever shall observe and teach them (the commands)
Shall be prominent in my sheepfold forever."

Miss Petite understood what the Shepherd was saying,
But she couldn't see herself
As the greatest in the sheepfold.
She just knew the Shepherd meant
She had to teach the lessons He had given her
Over the next few months.
She must not change them to suit herself
And must encourage all the other sheep
To learn the lessons as they were taught.
So many lessons yet to learn!
How would she manage such a massive task?
Still, she determined in her heart to do exactly
As the Shepherd had said.

5. Matthew 5:19, Spirit Filled Life Bible, NKJV, Thomas Nelson Publishers Inc., Nashville, TN., 1991.

Chapter 13
HEART KNOWLEDGE

It was time for Miss Petite to decide
What her feelings were for M. LeGrand.
She knew the priority in her life
Was to do what the Shepherd wanted her to do.
M. LeGrand was still in her thoughts.
She had wanted to walk with him,
And help him get his many bells.
She had wanted him to get his wool combed out,
To have the mats, briars, burrs, and thorns removed,
And the mud washed from his underside.

It seemed lately that all Miss Petite could think on
Were the bad times,
When M. LeGrand seemed ungrateful and out of sorts.
He just wasn't himself and perhaps she was to blame.
Perhaps she enjoyed chastising herself
For the big sheep's ill temper.

She was going to put away those memories forever.
Never would she make reference to them again.
M. LeGrand would get his own bells from the Shepherd,
When he got around to it.
He could pick out his own then;
He certainly didn't need her help.
In fact, he had told everyone quite plainly

To leave him alone.
He liked being alone.
Maybe other sheep didn't walk fast enough for him,
Or didn't carry on an interesting conversation,
Or maybe he didn't like to care for little sheep.

The Shepherd, on the other hand,
Had given Miss Petite everything M. LeGrand had.
She could talk to the Shepherd whenever she wished.
He taught her lessons about a caring love,
About walking at the rear of the flock,
And about avoiding bigger sheep that could be nasty and bite.
The Shepherd listened to all her troubles
And exciting daily encounters.
She began to list M. LeGrand's qualities
That resembled the Shepherd.
He was steady, firm and loving . . .

I Shall Not Want

The Shepherd interrupted Miss Petite.
"What are you doing, little sheep?
Are we back to the big sheep again?"

"Oh, my Dear Shepherd,
I am having difficulty sorting out in my mind
My feelings for M. LeGrand.
I am so mixed up.
Do you think you could help me, Dear Shepherd?
Are you displeased with me, Dear Shepherd?"

"Of course not, my little one.
It is natural for your mind to be on the big sheep.
Little sheep, do I love you?
And do I love the sheep of my flock?"

"Why yes, of course you do," she said.

"And where is my heart, little sheep?" the Shepherd asked.

"Dear Shepherd, your heart is always with us,
The sheep of the flock."

"Yes, dear little one, with the sheep I love,
And rightly so, for love is the heart."

"That's funny," she thought.
"The Shepherd had said before that
Love begins in the heart, not the mind.
And tonight, He said 'love is the heart.'"
Miss Petite began repeating the phrase over and over;
"Love is the heart, love is the heart, love is the heart."

Slowly the message began to dawn on her like
One of those bright stars above.
And Miss Petite began jumping for joy.
She jumped around in circles.
Then she did cartwheels and shouted with glee
At the top of her lungs.
She didn't care who she awakened.

She finally understood the Shepherd's message,
And understood her feelings for the big sheep.
Why had she tried to figure out with her mind,
What had begun in her heart?
She fell exhausted to the ground, and sang under the stars.

Chapter 14

REPENTANCE

M. LeGrand took Miss Petite along with him
To see the Shepherd.
She was excited that he had asked her to come
But she was apprehensive.
Was he going to ask for his wool to be brushed
Or bells to be hung around his neck?
M. LeGrand just loved the sound of the bells.
If he had his own, he would never have to
Ask the other sheep to play their bells again.
Miss Petite was sure that was it.
She danced excitedly alongside the big sheep.

M. LeGrand was more talkative than usual,
But it was only chatter.
He skipped around from subject to subject,
Excitable and flighty.
He usually looked at the Shepherd from a distance
Out of the corner of his eye,
So going directly to the Shepherd was
A big step for him.
When they neared the Shepherd,
M. LeGrand stopped Miss Petite
And sat her down on the pasture grass to wait.
He told her he wanted to speak to the Shepherd alone.

I Shall Not Want

The Shepherd was seated on a rock
And welcomed M. LeGrand when He saw him approaching.
Actually, the Shepherd had seen the big sheep coming
Since he had left the flock.
He had been waiting patiently.

Ordinarily quite composed in speech,
This time M. LeGrand garbled his words.
The Shepherd smiled as the big sheep
Shook his head and told the Shepherd
He would start over.
"Shepherd, sometimes we forget how matted we get
When walking in the flock.
We get careless about looking after ourselves.
We don't even see the briars, burrs and ticks in our wool.
Sometimes, these things cause hurt and pain to others
Even though they don't bother us.
We walk through mud and lie down in sloppy places,
Instead of taking care to lie down in green pasture.
We often end up quite messy on the outside."
The Shepherd never uttered a word,
But grinned at all the "we's" thrown in M. LeGrand's plea.
He took a quick glance over at Miss Petite
And chuckled to Himself,
As He had been keeping the little sheep
Clean and tidy everyday.

"Shepherd, I want you to shear me!"

At this, the Shepherd's eyes went wide. "Shear you my son?!"
"Yes", the big sheep answered, "Shear me now, please!"
The Shepherd would have laughed
But He realized the big sheep was serious,
So He talked quietly and gently to M. LeGrand.
"It is the wrong season to be shorn.
If I do it now, you could be bruised or hurt
Because there would be no wool to protect you.
Now is not the time to be shorn;
You will catch a cold."

I Shall Not Want

M. LeGrand interrupted.
"I am a mess, Shepherd!
I don't like the look of my wool anymore.
I want it cleaned up now!"

"Could I just brush you out?" the Shepherd asked.
He assured him that he could look like new
If He would just let Him brush him out.
And not jeopardize his health.

M. LeGrand was impatient and frazzled.
He spoke some words out of the book
That the Shepherd had given him a long time ago.
"Remember Shepherd, You said if we ask anything…"

He stopped because his memory did not serve him well.
The Shepherd held the big sheep's head in His hands
And looked him straight in the eyes.
"What is acceptable may not necessarily be the best, my son."

"But You tell us to keep clean
And if we get things in our wool
We are to come to you Shepherd," M. LeGrand protested.

"That is quite correct, big sheep.
You are to come and I can tell you, or show you
The best way to take care of the matter.
I am telling you, big sheep,
There is no need for you to be shorn.
You have only to let me brush you.
Do you realize that besides all those other reasons
I have given to you,
That if you went back to the flock with no wool
They would laugh at you?
They'd not spare anything for your feelings.
Could you bear that, big sheep?"

Still insisting, the big sheep went on.
"But you sheared the little sheep

When it wasn't the right season, Shepherd,
And none of the sheep laughed at her."

"Oh, but my son, the little sheep was sick
And could not carry the weight of the wool.
Instead of sending her back to the flock
To sleep on the cold nights or
To walk during the day when she might get briars,
I kept her in the pasture where the grass is green and soft.
Big sheep, you are not in the same situation as the little sheep.
You will be returning to the flock,
But if you insist I shear you, I will do it.
You will become ill and will have to spend time in the pasture.
Listen to me, please, my son.
I do not want to do anything to hurt you.
I am simply warning you of the dangers," the Shepherd finished.

M. LeGrand sat down on his haunches.
He didn't know what to do.
He turned and looked at the little sheep,
Then excused himself from the Shepherd
And went to speak to Miss Petite.

M. LeGrand explained to her that he wanted to be shorn
Rather than brushed,
But the Shepherd had advised against it.
"Well, big sheep, I think you should go back
And explain to Him exactly what you want and why.
Maybe the Shepherd didn't hear or understand you.
Never mind, I'll go and talk to Him for you.
He spends much time with me and I come to Him all the time.
Let me go to Him for you."
Miss Petite ran off to the Shepherd
To plead M. LeGrand's case;
To be shorn or to be combed out.
The Shepherd was very firm on His stand.
There was no need for the big sheep to be sheared.
He would brush him and remove the nasty things,
Bathe him and oil him,
And he would be as new.

I Shall Not Want

For the first time in a long time,
Miss Petite, in pleading the case for M. LeGrand,
Had swayed in loyalty;
She had rebelled just a shade against the Shepherd.

Her heart snapped back to the straight path
When M. LeGrand asked her what the Shepherd had said.
She explained that she had to agree with the Shepherd.
It was not the season to be sheared.
She tried to cajole him and tell him
How beautiful he looked,
Even with all those sticks poking out of his wool,
But that he would look even better once the Shepherd
Bathed him and put oil on him.

The big sheep stood erect and gasped: "What?!
Bathed and oiled? Not me!
That is for sissies and lady sheep!
The Shepherd isn't going to do that to me!
He can maybe brush me out, but that is all,
Absolutely all He can do!"

The little sheep took two steps back,
Surprised and hurt by M. LeGrand's reaction.
Why didn't he trust the Shepherd, even yet?
She wanted to cry and get angry all at once with M. LeGrand.
She wanted to walk away from him and say, "Ok. Do it your way!"

M. LeGrand must have noticed the hurt on Miss Petite's face,
And he came up to her carefully and snuggled in.
"Little sheep," he said, "can you realize I am a big sheep,
And the others in the flock know me as I am?
If I got bathed and oiled, they'd make fun of me.
They'd notice such a difference
That I am not sure I could take it.
I would like it if the Shepherd forgot about all those extras."

"But, M. LeGrand, you were willing to get sheared,
And the Shepherd explained all the sheep would laugh at you,
And still you were willing to do that. Why?" asked Miss Petite.

The big sheep thought for a long time and said,
"Well, little sheep, that is what I prepared myself for.
I could tell the other sheep I had asked the Shepherd for the shearing,
Not because I needed it, but because I wanted it.
If the Shepherd bathes me and oils me,
Every sheep in the flock will know it is because
The Shepherd had decided the treatment.
I couldn't take that, little sheep.
Not me. I'm a big sheep.
Please try to understand.
I do love you."

Miss Petite was sad;
Sad for the big sheep and for the Shepherd.
If only M. LeGrand could understand
How good the Shepherd could make him look and feel,
If he could only lose the fear of what others think.
Getting sheered had nothing to do with love.
Wait a minute. He actually said, "I love you!"
What a mixture of emotions!

"Big sheep, you know it's time for me to go back
To the flock before the Shepherd moves me to another place.
I cannot walk beside you with all that garbage in your wool."

The little sheep shuddered at her own words.
It wasn't exactly what she had meant.
She feared M. LeGrand would lash out
And he would have the right to do so,
But he looked sideways at her
Realizing she already felt remorse.

"Just the same," the big sheep thought, "the little sheep is right.
It is garbage and I don't want all these things
In my wool anymore.'

I Shall Not Want

M. LeGrand dropped Miss Petite off at her shelter
And Miss Petite went inside by herself and sat in a corner.
"It is useless to try to persuade M. LeGrand
To go get brushed out by the Shepherd.
He doesn't care about the Shepherd;
He doesn't care about me,
And he doesn't care about himself," she whined.

The little sheep was no longer hurt.
She was angry and stomped her hooves
On the floor of the shelter,
Disturbing some other sheep around her.
Some came to see what the trouble was,
And she shouted out loud
So every sheep could hear.
"The big sheep went to the Shepherd,
And was so obnoxious he wouldn't even listen,
And baa, baa, baa . . ."

Some sheep agreed with M. LeGrand,
And at those sheep, Petite sputtered
Even more vile things.

Then quietly, Promise (the lady sheep with the book),
Came to the door and asked to come in.
Miss Petite was totally embarrassed.
She knew she had no business saying anything
About M. LeGrand's conversation with the Shepherd.
She wondered if Promise had heard.
"Oh, she must have heard.
There is no way she wouldn't have heard all those
Nasty things I have just said," the little sheep muttered to herself.

Miss Petite motioned for Promise
To come and sit down beside her.
She did not accuse Miss Petite, but sat quietly.
At first Miss Petite wanted to change subjects;
Talk about the weather, or something.
Finally, she just burst into tears,
And fell down in front of Promise
Crying, "I'm sorry! I'm so sorry! Please forgive me!"

Still, Promise remained silent,
And helped Miss Petite to her feet,
Instructing her to sit beside her.
She opened her book and asked Miss Petite
To read along with her.

I Shall Not Want

"Judge not that you be not judged;
For with what judgment you judge,
You will be judged;
And with the measure you use,
It will be measured back to you.
And do you look at the speck in your brother's eye,
But do not consider the plank in your own eye?" (6)
Promise put her book down,
And Miss Petite was feeling ashamed;
Not because she accused her of anything,
But because the little sheep couldn't pretend any longer
And told Promise everything she had done.
She listened, but graciously explained
That Miss Petite didn't owe an apology to her,
But to M. LeGrand.
The little sheep bolted out the door to apologize to the big sheep
Before dark,
Leaving Promise in her dust.

Delighted, Miss Petite ran as fast as she could
To see M. LeGrand standing
So big and strong,
Allowing the Shepherd to brush out his wool.
The Shepherd welcomed her to sit and watch.
He was extremely gentle,
And spoke softly to the big sheep
As He combed and pulled.
Sometimes he would wince
When the Shepherd pulled too hard,
But he remained standing tall, straight
And proud.

At one point the Shepherd came to whisper
In Miss Petite's ear
That He would need her to calmly reassure M. LeGrand
While the Shepherd pulled a thorn from his flesh.
The big sheep began to squirm,
But the little sheep talked of the Shepherd's love.
This was not difficult for her
And she went on and on

I Shall Not Want

About how the Shepherd had looked after her,
And built a shelter, and an open fire,
And how much the Shepherd loved her.

The Shepherd had to reach over and touch her
So she would stop talking.
Embarrassed, she thought she would begin
Her trek home, before darkness fell.
The Shepherd would be combing out
The big sheep the next day as well.
She had made a few steps home,
When she remembered why she had come
In the first place.
Shamefacedly, she returned.
"Is there something on your mind,
Little sheep?" the Shepherd spoke.
"Yes, Dear Shepherd.
I do need to apologize to the big sheep."
M. LeGrand never batted an eye,
But waited for her to continue.

"You see, Dear Shepherd,
When the big sheep didn't stay with You
To get the wool brushed,
I said all kinds of nasty things about him to many sheep.
I'm sure every sheep in the pasture and the flock
Could have heard me.
Some came by to tell me they had heard
And they had agreed with me.
But that still wasn't right, Dear Shepherd."

Miss Petite moved over to stand
Directly in front of M. LeGrand.
"I'm sorry, big sheep, for not being more understanding,
Caring and loving.
I'm sorry of accusing you of having ticks and burrs
In your wool, when I have the same in mine.
I just noticed I have a stick under my chin,
And I have never noticed a stick in your wool, ever.
Would you pull it out for me, please?"

The big sheep looked at the little sheep and kindly said,
"I'd really like to take that stick out
From under your chin because I know it must bother you,
But if I do that, I will jiggle
And the Shepherd has told me to stand still.
Why don't you go around to the side of me
And have the Shepherd remove it for you? He will, I know."
So she moved around to the Shepherd,
Opened her mouth,
And the Shepherd pulled the stick out.
Miss Petite said goodnight.
She heard M. LeGrand call out to her,
"Sleep under the stars tonight, little sheep,
And look to the sky. Rest well, my little one."

"My little one," thought Miss Petite.
That was an endearing term
The Shepherd always used with her.

6. Matthew 7:1-3, Spirit Filled Life Bible, NKJV, Thomas Nelson Publishers Inc., Nashville, TN., 1991.

Chapter 15

THE BOOK, THE BELL AND THE HEART

"M. LeGrand, why don't you admit it?
Admit your love for Miss Petite!"
The familiar voice came from behind.

"What? What are you talking about?"
LeGrand screeched, turning to see who spoke,
And recognizing him, turned his back again.

" I am Nobody, but I know you love Miss Petite.
Why can't you accept that?"

"Listen, Mr. Nobody," he said emphatically;
"You don't know what you are talking about,
And I don't wish to discuss it with you."

"Alright, M. LeGrand, but I am right, and you know it!" said Nobody.

With that, LeGrand stood tall and strong, running
From the place of Solitude, up and over the ditch and across the bridge.
He remembered the bridge was the place
He had thrown away his bell.

He spotted it, lying half covered with water,
Picked it up and ran to the mound in the meadow,

Shaking the bell, crying and screaming,
"No sheep is going to tell me I love the little sheep.
Who did that sheep think he was?
Why would he push his nose into my business?
Who said he could speak to me?
I was sitting there, ready to read
What the Shepherd had asked me to read and . . ."
He stopped in dead silence.

The book!
He had left it lying in the place of Solitude in the pasture.
This infuriated him even more,
And he raged, shaking and ringing his bell hard and loud,
So no one would hear all the nasty things he had to say.
He cried and cried, hating everything around him.

Cautiously, the Shepherd approached him.
The other sheep rushed over to the clanging of the bell,
To witness the spectacle.
The Shepherd waved to them to leave,
And they moved calmly, though still curious.
They had never seen M. LeGrand act like this.
The Shepherd took hold of M. LeGrand's front legs,
Which were waving and swinging the bell frantically.

M. LeGrand opened his eyes, and through the blur
He could see the tender look of the Shepherd.
He broke and fell down in front of Him crying.
"You were so kind, Dear Shepherd, to brush me out.
I was so clean! Now look what I have done!
I have spoken harshly about You,
About Miss Petite,
And Mr. Nobody.
You asked me to read Your book,
But I've gone running off, leaving it
In the place of Solitude.
Dear Shepherd, I am so ashamed,
So embarrassed!
Why can I not do better?
Dear Shepherd, I have always been in control.

I have never lost control in my whole life!
I control circumstances; they do not control me!
Please, Dear Shepherd, will you help me?"

The Shepherd moved directly in front of LeGrand.
He knelt down, picked him up off the ground,
"Big sheep, my beloved,
There is no need to scold you;
You have asked for forgiveness."
He continued.
"As for your outburst, big sheep,
That is only natural; you are hurt,
But remember, I will not leave you alone.
It is important for you to spend time reading My book now.
If you don't, you will become more depressed.
Please do not dwell on the past.
Read my book and study the lessons well.
I will help you as you go."

I Shall Not Want

The Shepherd dried off the book
And opened it to a portion He wanted him to read.
"Take your time, big sheep.
Read it thoroughly. It will help you get your mind off yourself."

M. LeGrand sat up and looked the Shepherd squarely in the face.
He burst out, "I cannot think of anything but the little sheep!
She was such a nuisance, and I did not wish to take care of her.
I cared for her in my heart,
But I did not wish to love her, Dear Shepherd."

The Shepherd looked directly in his eyes.
"Why not, big sheep, have you thought of that?"

"Yes, I have, Dear Shepherd. Would you like me to tell you now?"

"Yes, big sheep. Let us talk about it now,
While we are alone in the meadow.
There is no one to hear our conversation.
Tell me, please."

M. LeGrand was not accustomed
To sharing his inner feelings.
He didn't feel it was necessary,
To do as others did.
But he wanted to now.
The Shepherd was the only one he could trust.

The Shepherd made a fire,
And heated some herbal tea.
M. LeGrand was grateful for the attention,
And began to relax and talk freely.
"Why is it necessary
To admit I love the little sheep?"

The Shepherd stopped him.
"Big sheep, my beloved, I have already told you
That I would like you to go on some missions with Me.
There are errands for you to carry out.
If you cannot love,

Or admit to loving someone close to you?
How can you go to other sheep
And tell them I love them?
For if you cannot tell them and show them
You love them, They will not believe that I love them.
Do you understand, big sheep?"

M. LeGrand became sullen
And hesitated for a very long time.

"Big sheep, I will leave you now.
When you are ready, I have a surprise for you."
As the Shepherd was leaving across the bridge,
He turned back to say
"Big sheep, remember please,
Do not let your fire go out.
And return to the pasture
As soon as you can."

M. LeGrand had never looked at things
This way before;
Of course he loved the little sheep.
He hated to admit it.
But now, for the first time,
The Shepherd had pointed out a new thought.
He couldn't go on a mission
With a closed heart,
A heart whose fire had gone out.

How could he be ready for the surprise?
What did he have to do?
He began reading the book
Where the Shepherd had opened it.
It was about loving the brethren.
"For where envying and strife is,
There is confusion and every evil work."

"Is that what the little sheep was talking about?
One cannot have jealousy, envy and strife
Along with love?
Oh, little sheep, if you were here, I would tell you I loved you.
With love there is no fear,
So I would be fearless in telling you, little sheep."

He sat up straight and called out;
To the meadow, "I love you."
To the trees, "I love you."
To the one shining star,
He reached out his front legs,
And bleated loudly,
As though the star might hear him,
"Mr. Star, I love you!"
At the top of his voice he shouted: "I love you, little sheep, my beloved."

Chapter 16

THE LESSONS

M. LeGrand called on Miss Petite,
But didn't have much to say.
Early on in the conversation
She had asked him a question,
But he had not bothered to answer.
She had chattered on
And forgot herself what question was asked.
As soon as the big sheep had said hello,
He had also said goodbye.
Not a permanent goodbye,
Just a detached
"I love you and want you to know I do care,
Even though I never talk to you."

Somehow, Miss Petite never got used
To that kind of conversation.
Her inner instinct had always been,
"If you love me, show me.
Put actions behind your words
Whether it is of love, joy or peace.
Every thought should have actions.
Wasn't that what the book said?
'What does it profit, my brethren,
If someone says he has faith but does not have works?'" (7)

I Shall Not Want

As soon as the conversation was over,
Miss Petite flopped down in the pasture
Confused and disgruntled.
She should have been pleased that
M. LeGrand had come to her to talk this time.
In fact there had been many visitors today.
Miss Bow (with the pink ribbon)
And Bumper with all the tiny sheep
Had come to plan next Friday's meeting,
To study the book together.

"Why is it," Miss Petite thought,
"That I am so good at telling other sheep
What and how and when to do things?
I never tell them to their faces;
(Well, not always and not often.)
But I can tell them all the answers to their questions.
I can tell them how to manage their affairs
And how to avoid situations which might bring trouble."

She remembered the episode with Promise
And the lesson on the speck and the plank
In the eye of judgment.
She certainly hadn't appreciated
Criticism by other sheep.
She discovered when she was being criticized,
It was actually a spear in the Shepherd's side.
"Oh!" the little sheep shuddered.
"I would never want to criticize the Shepherd."
She wanted to crawl under the shelter and hide.

Meanwhile, the Shepherd passed by,
And Miss Petite called out
"I'm sorry, Shepherd!"

He stopped, looking stern,
And asked her what she was talking about.
"If you are truly sorry, do something about it.
Put actions behind your words."

Miss Petite's mouth fell open.
She couldn't believe it.
The Shepherd had used the same word
She had used to judge M. LeGrand.
She sank to the floor, crushed.
"Obviously," she said to herself,
"The Shepherd must want me to apologize
To the big sheep for judging him.
Doesn't He know that the big sheep
Should be apologizing to me?
After all, M. LeGrand had been mean to me
Way back . . ."
The little sheep stopped.
"You know, I really can't remember when
And I can't remember what he did
But I remember it was downright awful!"

She went on talking to herself;
"Dear Shepherd, let me remind You
That this is a two-way street
And the big sheep is bottling up the traffic.
Mr. Shepherd, I don't want to apologize to M. LeGrand
And I don't think I should have to.
I don't even want him around any more.
I don't need him, I don't look for him
And I certainly don't wait for him to drop by or call."
"Mr. Shepherd, the big sheep has not even come
To see my new shelter.
He doesn't know how the other sheep hurt me with their comments
When I was sick.
How critical they were;
How misunderstanding;
How they butted their noses
Where they didn't belong.
They hurt me and I still hurt.
None of those sheep came to apologize to me
For criticizing my actions and behavior.
Not one came to say they were sorry.
Not even those who love You, Mr. Shepherd."
Miss Petite's lip was so low it was touching the floor.

I Shall Not Want

She didn't care who knew she was pouting.
She was sure that the Shepherd did not have all the facts.

Miss Petite left the shelter and curled up under a leafy tree.
The breeze made the leaves tremble
And flipped the pages in her book.
She wished she could read her book that fast.

She looked more closely at the leaves on the tree,
Examining their color, shape and the way
Each moved differently in the breeze.
They were different in every possible way,
But they all came from one trunk.
She thought of them as sheep.
"As each leaf on this tree is different,
So is each sheep different
Even when the sheep loves the Shepherd.
We are all sheep,
That is what we have in common.
We all have a Shepherd, though not all love Him,
But we initially come from Him.
Some leaves are closer to the trunk than others.
Some are out on top enjoying the sun and rain
And can take weather beatings,
While others stay protected underneath."

Miss Petite looked at the pages of her book,
Blown open by the wind...
"But also for this very reason, giving all diligence,
Add to your faith virtue, to virtue knowledge,
To knowledge self-control, to self-control..." (8)

Virtue meant having moral goodness, good quality or inherent power.
"No, I failed that one. I never got past the first step."
Knowledge meant all that is or may be known.
"Had I really listened
To what the big sheep had been saying when he called,
I would have understood why he called on me.
I was so busy talking myself, I didn't understand.
I failed this too."

Self-control meant that which guides conduct.
She had thrown such a tantrum,
Exhibited such complete loss of self-control
That it embarrassed her to think on it.
No wonder the Shepherd was displeased.
He had every right to show His anger.

Miss Petite wanted to close her book
And never open it again.
"If this is going to show me all the bad things about me
Then I'm not really interested," she muttered.
"I used to open this book and see promises
From the Shepherd.
Now, all I see are words of instruction!
Do this, don't do that!"

Still, she knew that the pages
Had been blown open there for a reason.
"Probably the Shepherd blew the breeze
To make the pages open there," she muttered again.

Patience meant bearing trials without murmuring, the quality of enduring.
"Patience?" she screeched.
"Who has been more patient than I, when it comes to M. LeGrand?
Have I not waited for him to get cleaned up?
Have I not waited for him to get his bells?
Have I not waited to walk beside him?
Well, I sure am not going to walk beside him now
Even if he does get cleaned up or gets hundreds of bells around his neck.
Never!"

Miss Petite stopped abruptly.
"Dear Shepherd, do I have to go through
This list again, from the beginning?
Will I never learn?"

She dropped to the ground,
Buried her head,
And wept.

Her whole insides hurt
From a deep cutting pain inside.
"Ouch!" the little sheep squealed.
There was the Shepherd,
Holding a long thorn
That had gone through the little sheep's flesh.
How long it was!
Where had she picked that up from?
It would take time for that wound to heal.

"Little sheep," the Shepherd said softly;
"Have you done a lesson for today yet?"

Shamefully, the little sheep lowered her head
And looked to the ground.
"Yes, Dear Shepherd. It wasn't one I planned to do,
But the breeze blew the pages open in the book for me.
Dear Shepherd, I am so very sorry
For judging one of Your sheep;
A sheep I know you love very much.
I am sorry for judging You too,
For I am very much aware that You know all things.
Will You help me to be more like You?"

The Shepherd replied, "Little sheep, if you love me,
Keep, (*seize, preserve, possess and grasp*) my commandments.
That you shall love the Lord, (*your Shepherd*),
With all your heart, with all your soul,
With all your mind.
This is the first and great commandment.
And the second is like it:
You shall love your neighbor as yourself, (*little sheep*)." (9)

The Shepherd continued:
"'A new commandment I give to you, (*little sheep*):
That you love one another;
As I have loved you,
That you also love one another.
By this all will know that you are My disciples (*belonging to me*),
If you have love for one another."(10)

I Shall Not Want

Miss Petite was delighted.
Nothing would please her more
Than to have everyone know that she
Belonged to the Good Shepherd
Who had done so much for her.
She truly did love Him.

The Shepherd had to be on His way.
He had to visit a very sick sheep
In the pasture that evening.
Miss Petite apologized again for her behavior.

The little sheep began composing a letter.
"My Dearest Friend, Big Sheep:
I do love you and thank you for calling in on me today.
Thank you for the few minutes we talked together,
Even though I recognized later
That most of the chatter came from me.
Forgive me for not listening to you properly.
The lesson I learned from the Shepherd today
Was about love; attributes I see in you.
You have shown love to the Shepherd,
To me, and to the miserable sheep in the flock.
Big sheep, would you show me
How to love with such depth?
Help me to let things pass over without getting insulted.
Help me not to look to others to follow them,
But to walk beside them to learn.
Would you allow me to walk beside you
That I might learn and ask questions?
I would always keep my eye on the Shepherd.
Thank you for being understanding,
Caring and loving toward me, big sheep.
The Lord bless you and keep you.
The Lord make His face shine upon you,
And be gracious to you.
The Lord lift up His countenance upon you
And give you peace."
Your friend, the little sheep.

7. James 2:14, <u>Spirit Filled Life Bible</u>, **NKJV**, Thomas Nelson Inc.,Nashville,TN., USA. 1991.
8. Ibid., 2 Peter 1:5-6.
9. Ibid., Matthew 22:37-38
10. Ibid., John 13:34.

Chapter 17

FOG AND CONFUSION

Miss Petite could see nothing
When she looked out her tower window.
The fog had persisted for days.
She hadn't ventured out of her shelter
For fear of getting lost.
The cold and damp penetrated her wool.
She stared at the wall hanging the Shepherd had given her.
Maybe she could use it as a blanket.

She could barely make out images
Of sheep not far from her shelter.
She was concerned for them
Out there in the damp mist without a cover.
The other flocks were invisible,
Nor could she hear their bleating;
In fact, she had not heard the bleating at all
In these fogged-in days.

Wait! There was a faint sound of music,
Somewhere off in the distance,
But where?
Fog distorted sight and sound.
It could sound like it was coming from the right
And actually be coming from the left.
It could sound like a trumpet

And only be a flute.
Miss Petite laughed.
She remembered the stories in the Shepherd's book
About the angels who blew trumpets.
If she heard the music,
It would have to be a trumpet.
This was no trumpet blast, only a flute.
Could the fog distort sound that much?

The little sheep sat down in the upper level of her shelter
And pretended she was the one hearing the trumpet blast,
The calling of the Lord,
And how she would so nobly respond to the call.

She knew the trumpet would only have to sound once.
Why, she could go before the trumpet could finish His call.
She envisioned the Shepherd placing a purple robe
Upon her back, patting her head and saying
"Well done, little sheep.
You have responded valiantly to the call of the trumpet."

Oh, Miss Petite was thrilled and relived that scene,
Over and over again.

She dozed off for awhile, only to be
Awakened suddenly by a faint cry
And knocking on the wall of her shelter.
Looking out her upper level window
She could see nothing.
Miss Petite called out,
"What's wrong?
What are you looking for?
Do you need something?"

There was no answer.
It mustn't have been very serious, she thought.
Probably a sheep that lost his way
And bumped into the shelter; that was all.
She leaned against the post by the ramp
And heard the same cry.

This time it was muffled and disturbed.
"Is there someone out there?
Are you hungry? Cold?
Lost?"

Still no answer came,
So Miss Petite sat down feeling the chill,
And smiled at how the fog had come in
Like a blanket;
But not warm like the one on her wall.
She was troubled by the incidents of the last few minutes,
Wishing she could block out the sound
As they replayed in her head.
Miss Petite felt restless in the eerie atmosphere.
She tried to read the stories,
But the closed shutters darkened the room.
Then, she tried to recite stories she had memorized.

She liked the one about being in Heaven with the Good Shepherd.
There was no more trouble, only streets of gold
And glorious singing.
Maybe some day she would hear a trumpet blast,
And meet an angel!

She hopped up straight out of her sprawled position.
"What on earth was that?
There seemed to be a lot of confusion out there in the fog.

I Shall Not Want

Miss Petite hurried down her ramp
And around to the back of her shelter
Where she had first heard the noises.
She could barely see in front of her
But knelt down to search with her hooves.
There was a tiny whimper.
Following the sound,
She cleared away some dirt and tall grass
And there, in a small thorn bush,
She found a tiny lamb.

Miss Petite gently lifted the lamb.
Even in the fog she could see the cuts and sores.
She spoke softly to the lamb assuring him,
As she carried him inside the shelter.
She bathed his sores
Just as the Shepherd had done for her
Many times before.
The lamb was emaciated,
So Miss Petite warmed up her leftover portions
Over the open fire.
The lamb was grateful and told Miss Petite
That he had been sick and lost his way
In his search for the Shepherd.
He shivered as he talked.
Miss Petite snuggled in close to try to warm him.
The hanging rug caught her eye,
So she pulled it from the wall and wrapped it around the lamb.
"Oh, this is beautiful. Where did you get it?"

"The Shepherd gave it to me some time ago," said the little sheep.
"Only, I have never used it except for a wall hanging."

The lamb snuggled down in the rug-blanket
And fell fast asleep.
Miss Petite sat by his side for hours keeping him company,
Even though the lamb didn't need her,
Or know she was there.

I Shall Not Want

Many hours later, the Shepherd walked in.
"I knew you'd look after this lamb, little sheep."

"What do you mean?" asked Miss Petite.

"Well, you see, there were two other sheep
Who got lost in the fog earlier tonight.
When I found them, they were already dead.
They must have banged themselves pretty hard on something,
Because they had head wounds and other lacerations.
The lamb was obviously heading in the same direction,
And I knew unless someone stopped him,
We'd lose him too." The Shepherd paused.

"Little sheep, it breaks my heart to see these sheep
Wandering where they're not supposed to.
I had prepared a special pen for all of them;
A place to stay during this heavy fog.
Two decided to go their own way and
This little one decided to follow.
Thank you so much for saving this little one."

The Shepherd went over to the lamb,
Removed the blanket and placed it around Miss Petite.
The underside of the blanket was rich purple.
He had put it on her like a robe.
She looked down at herself in total amazement and said,
"Dear Shepherd, I don't deserve this purple robe.
I really don't."

"Little sheep, this lamb you didn't know
Was a stranger.
You brought him into your shelter.
He was sick, hungry, thirsty and cold,
And you fed and clothed him.
You put your own special rug around him
That you had not used yet yourself.
He had been caught up in the brambles,
And you loosed him.
You did not care about getting cut or bruised yourself.

Little sheep, what you did for this tiny sheep,
You actually did for Me.
You deserve the purple robe."

The Shepherd picked up the lamb,
Carrying him out the door.
As He passed Miss Petite,
He bent down and touched the open cut on her leg,
And whispered, "Be healed."

Miss Petite sat stunned for a long while.
She was not worthy of the purple robe.
She wondered if the other two sheep lost in the fog
Had been the ones that she had heard outside her shelter.
She had called but hadn't understood
What they were saying.
She gasped. "No wonder they didn't answer!
They were too injured to speak, to even make sense.
All I did was call out.
I even closed the shutters so I wouldn't have to hear them.
They needed me.
Maybe they were looking for the Shepherd.
They were lost."
Now Miss Petite became distraught
Because she had not made a move to save
The crying sheep.

"I just looked from my tower!
Who can see anything from a tower?
You have to come down to ground level
To see the tiny flowers in the grass.
One must walk the path to feel it under foot.
One must eat the grass to know its taste.
My tower, my lookout!
The Shepherd built it for me.
He must have had a better use for it than I had thought.
He would never have wanted me in the tower
At the cost of losing two sheep."

I Shall Not Want

Miss Petite took off her purple robe
And hung it with the purple side next to the wall
So she wouldn't have a constant memory
Of this night's events.

Chapter 18

A FOGGY DAY

As soon as the fog lifted,
Miss Petite went in search of the Shepherd.
He had been searching
For lost sheep during these days of fog.
Miss Petite slipped her book on to her collar,
Then realized why the Shepherd had not
Given her a bell as well.
The weight of just the book caused great pain,
A remembrance of the illness so long ago.
She stopped to rest.

A sick sheep noticed the book on her collar.
"What is that hanging from your collar?"

Suddenly, Miss Petite was embarrassed,
For she had never taken this book outside of her house.
What if he laughed when she told him
It was a book from the Shepherd?
If she tried to lie and say it was something else,
The sheep would not believe her.
The book had a distinct appearance from any other.
She pretended to be hard of hearing.
The question came again.
"Oh, it's really nothing; it's something I found along the way,"
The little sheep said.

I Shall Not Want

"Oh, I thought it was a book from the Shepherd
And I was going to ask if I could borrow it," the other sheep persisted.

Now what would she say?
She couldn't change her mind now; she would be caught in a lie.
She couldn't pretend she just found it; she would look stupid.
Instead, she ignored him, got up and staggered on her way.

Why did this encounter tire her so?
She didn't want to loan out the book,
And still had many questions to ask the Shepherd.
She wanted Him to find some happy stories in the book.
"Do's and don'ts", that is all she was learning;
And getting plenty tired of that!
She wanted more promises from the Shepherd.

As she walked she thought about other sheep.
There were many who didn't follow the commandments of the Shepherd,
Yet, they still said they loved Him.
It didn't seem the Shepherd ever chastised them.
Why did He not contend with the other sheep?
Why was He always at her?
Miss Petite was walking with her head down
When she heard a sheep from the pasture call to her.

"Little sheep, is that not the book from the Shepherd?"
Without lifting her head to see who had spoken,
The little sheep nodded
And continued lugging one foot after the other.

Now the sheep from the pasture was right beside her;
"Little sheep! May I read the book from the Shepherd, please?"

Miss Petite stopped dead in her tracks,
Turning to look at the pursuer.
It was the same sheep that had questioned her earlier.
Where was she?
She had gone in a complete circle,
Having come back to exactly the same place

Where she had been earlier this morning.
"I must have been lost in thought," she said to herself.

Again the sheep pestered her;
"Little sheep, would you mind if I took a look
At the book the Shepherd gave you?"

"No, not at all," she, said, rolling her eyes.
She slipped it from her collar.
Miss Petite wanted to apologize for her lie earlier,
But knew the sick sheep was aware of that.
She handed him her book.
"I'm sorry. I know it is no excuse but I am so distraught.
The Shepherd taught me so many lessons from that book
And I just cannot handle anymore right now.
I have even walked myself around in a circle
Just from not being able to lift my head up
To see where I was going.
Please forgive me."

"Hi! I'm Shadow." He smiled broadly, and nodded.
"And you are?"
"Miss Petite," the little sheep said, sighing.

I Shall Not Want

"Miss Petite, I understand.
I am an old sheep now and about to die.
When I was young I had lots on my mind, too,
And no time for others."

"Did you also have a book from the Shepherd?
You seemed to recognize mine," asked Miss Petite.

"Oh, yes, the Shepherd has been a good friend of mine.
We used to walk together quite often,
And He would teach me many things.
But I, like you, got tired of learning
And decided I'd walk where I wanted to
And behave as I willed.
Don't get me wrong.
I didn't become wild,
I just continued to walk as the Shepherd taught me
And I never did anything out of place.
I just didn't learn any more lessons from the Shepherd."

"Did anything happen to you, my new friend?
Did the Shepherd punish you
For not going to Him for more lessons?
Did He use the crook around your neck?" Miss Petite inquired.

"Oh no, Miss Petite, the Shepherd loved me
And He knew I loved Him.
I was tired of aiming for 'perfection.'
I have missed being with the Shepherd,
Because through the years I have spoken to Him
Only when I needed help.
I have missed our sharing, His warmth."

Shadow looked out into the blanket of the fog.
"I have not been a problem to the Shepherd,
But neither have I been a help to Him.
I recall several times I could have gone
With Him to the aid of some younger sheep;
If only I had stood beside the Shepherd,
But I didn't.

I sat back and watched."
Sure, the Shepherd handled the young ones without my help,
But it would have been better
If I had stood strong beside Him.
No, the Shepherd didn't beat me
Or treat me mean because of my decision;
I just didn't grow any more."
Miss Petite looked down at Shadow.
"Grow? What did he mean grow?
He looked like one of the biggest sheep she had ever seen.
Of course he had grown," she thought to herself.

"Would you like to sit down beside me,
And tell me what the Shepherd has been teaching you?
I'd love to hear some of the old stories
He used to tell me.
I'm sure they haven't changed.
Start way back at the beginning,
If you would, please."

Miss Petite got excited.
"At the beginning, my new friend?
At the beginning?
I am afraid I can't.
I haven't read that much of my book yet!
Well, you see, uh . . . I mean . . .
I haven't read that part of my book yet."
She began to blush.

"Oh, I am sorry, little sheep.
When I was your age,
I did exactly the same thing.
I read all the interesting and funny stories.
It wasn't until I grew up that I started to read the book
From cover to cover," Shadow smiled weakly.

"You've read the book cover to cover, my new friend?"

"Oh yes, Miss Petite, many, many times."

"And you still learned lessons, and more that you didn't want to learn?
Wouldn't you learn everything the first time you read the book?"

"No, little sheep, it doesn't matter how many times
You read this book.
You will always find something new in it.
There will always be new lessons.
When I decided I didn't want any more lessons,
I left my book behind.
I didn't really want to read it anymore.
But I've never forgotten its true value.
I am so glad you came along this morning with this book."

Miss Petite butted in;
"I know a lady sheep who has read her book over and over.
She showed me some new things in her book the other day.
I didn't like her lesson much, either.
I'll go get her and I know she would be glad to bring you up to date.
She could tell you all the lessons you missed
And all the ones you should learn before you die!"
Miss Petite gulped and bowed her head.

"Oh no, little sheep, that'll be fine," the sick sheep said.
"You see, the lady sheep will learn her lessons,
As I must learn mine
And you will learn yours.
We don't all learn the same lessons,
Or in the same order
Or at the same time."

"Well, Shadow, why don't I tell you about the Shepherd's love?"

Miss Petite always loved to talk
About how the Shepherd loved His sheep,
And cared for them;
How He'd use the crook if He needed to,
And how He'd give the sheep anything
They asked for,
If they loved Him and kept His commandments.

I Shall Not Want

"That will be just fine if you'd do that, little sheep.
Here, help me get comfortable and I'll just lie back
And listen to you," Shadow said
As he stretched out and prepared to listen.

Miss Petite sat down, looking up at the sky
And talked on and on
As though she were talking to the Shepherd Himself.
She didn't know how long she had been there
With Shadow, before the Shepherd came along.

"Oh, my Dear Shepherd, You are here —
I am so glad," she blurted out.
"I met Shadow from the pasture here,
And he asked me to tell him about the things
You taught me from Your book.
I've been telling him about Your love
And how we learn to love just like You.
Isn't it wonderful, Dear Shepherd?"

"Yes, my little one, it is wonderful."
The Shepherd knelt over Shadow,
Wrapped His cloak around him
And lifted him into His arms.

"Where are You going, Dear Shepherd?
What are You doing?
Why are You taking Shadow away?
He's been listening to my stories.
He wants to hear about Your love.
What are You doing?" she said, getting worried.

"Little sheep, you have made this sheep very happy
During his last moments in the pasture.
Thank you for that.
I am taking him home with me now.
Don't cry, little sheep, he will be fine.
There is a special place for sheep like this one."

The Shepherd paused, and then continued.
"Little sheep, always remember
What Shadow has taught you this day."

And then the Shepherd left
With Shadow in his arms.
Miss Petite cried and cried,
Because she had just made a new friend this morning,
And now, by early afternoon, he had been taken from her.
She wept all the way back to her shelter.
She hurt too much to tell anyone and needed to be by herself.
Time would heal this inside hurt.
Had she made him comfortable enough?
Could she have done more for him?
What about a drink, a special treat?
Perhaps the stories were a special treat.
What had the Shepherd meant when He said,
"Always remember what Shadow has taught you today."

"Wasn't I the one who told him the lessons of love
From the book of the Shepherd?"
But she hurt too much to think on it any longer.

Chapter 19

COMFORT AND FRIENDSHIP

Miss Petite was still mourning the loss
Of her new friend, Shadow,
When M. LeGrand came knocking at her door.
He didn't enter, but quietly and politely
Asked her if he could come and sit by the fire
And talk for awhile before the dew fell.
She was exhausted from her day's experience
But glad to have his company.

She took down her wall hanging
And gave it to M. LeGrand to put on the ground as a carpet.
She joined him and they watched the glow of the fire
Together.
The night air was cool but fresh.
The birds had gone to their nests,
And there was the sound of a few crickets.
Neither spoke.

The Shepherd's footsteps could be heard
As He made his rounds.
He passed by at one point and spoke to them.
"Good evening. I see you two are finally together."

M. LeGrand smiled at the Shepherd,
And Miss Petite grunted "yaaa"
But kept looking at the fire.
Then He continued on His Way.

The stars began to twinkle brightly,
And M. LeGrand helped Miss Petite
To her feet and escorted her to the shelter.
He wrapped the rug around her
And helped her to open the door.
Without protest, she went in, turning to say goodnight.
LeGrand closed in and rubbed his nose on hers,
And smiling said, "Have a good night, little sheep.
See you tomorrow."

She had a restless sleep,
Tossing and turning,
Thinking still of the new friend
Who was taken so quickly.

As she dozed, she could hear
Choirs of angels singing off in the distance.
She was sure it wasn't a flute or a trumpet,
But angel choirs.
She went to sleep dreaming
Of glorious angels.

Miss Petite was surprised early in the morning
By M. LeGrand standing at her door,
Calling her gently to get up.
He explained that he had stayed out by the fire all night
And kept it going.
"But," Miss Petite said, noticing she was wearing the robe,
"Without a cover, big sheep?
You must have been cold. Why did you not take this cover?"

"Oh, little sheep, you were so forlorn last night,
That I could not leave you.
I just had to stay to comfort you even though
You didn't know I was here.
You needed covering more than I did.
You needed to snuggle down and sleep properly.
Did you have a good sleep, little sheep?"

"Oh, yes, I dreamt of angel choirs singing in the heavens!"

M. LeGrand smiled, but said not a word,
For he too had heard the angel choirs singing
And was blessed by them.
Miss Petite offered to make some warm tea,
But M. LeGrand had already prepared breakfast.
"Little sheep, come. Look here!
I have already fixed us muffins and tea.
I hope you do not think I am too presumptuous."

"Not at all, big sheep. You are so good to me.
Why, no other sheep has ever treated me in such a manner.
And you stayed here all night?"
He could have stayed in the shelter,
But she didn't want to question the big sheep's judgment.

I Shall Not Want

Miss Petite wiped the sleep from her eyes.
She couldn't believe the transformation in M. LeGrand.
"Big sheep," she blurted out.
"You look absolutely wonderful.
What have you done to yourself?
You are beautiful!"
Even when M. LeGrand
Had briars, burrs and thistles in his wool,
She thought him beautiful.
(Oh, she could have bitten her tongue for saying that.)
But this was a different kind of beauty.
"Little sheep, this is what I came to talk to you about last night.
The Shepherd has been brushing me out.
It has taken Him a long time, but He is almost finished.
I decided to stay in the pasture for awhile."

"Oh," Miss Petite butted in;
"Why would you ever do that?
You'll miss those sheep over there,
Even if you don't talk to them very much.
Why would you want to stay in the pasture?
Don't you know the pasture is for sick and afflicted sheep?"

M. LeGrand shook his head and thought,
"Isn't that just like the little sheep?
How irritating she can be sometimes!"

Then he said, "No, little sheep, the pasture
Is not just for the sick and afflicted sheep.
The Shepherd keeps all kinds of sheep close to Him
In the pasture.
Sometimes He has sheep who have been led astray
By bigger or older sheep;
Sometimes sheep go astray themselves;
Sometimes sheep need to learn some lessons;
And sometimes sheep want to be with the Shepherd
For comfort, safety, and to learn.
Little sheep, you have seen only a small portion of the pasture
Where there are sick and afflicted sheep.
There is so much more for you to see!"

I Shall Not Want

"But big sheep, you haven't been here for very long.
How come you have seen so much more than me
And I wander through the pasture every day?"

Being facetious, M. LeGrand answered;
"I keep my eyes open."

Miss Petite let the comment pass.
"Well, then, are you staying in the pasture
To learn, or because you are sick
And haven't told me yet?
Why didn't you tell me this last night?"
"Little sheep, last night you seemed so forsaken,
I could not tell you anything.
When the Shepherd came by and spoke to us,
You couldn't even speak to him."

"The Shepherd? I didn't see the Shepherd last night?
I must have. He comes by every evening!
Big sheep, I must go see the Shepherd, right now!"

M. LeGrand set Miss Petite back down.
"Little sheep, the Shepherd is there in the pasture.
He will be there all day.
He knows you want to see Him.
He knows you didn't mean to ignore Him
And that you had a lot on your mind."

"I did. Yesterday morning, I made friends with a sick sheep,
And by early afternoon, he was taken from me.
I just felt so alone.
I don't know where he came from.
I do know he loved the Shepherd,
But he stopped learning a long time ago
Because it hurt so much."

M. LeGrand looked at Miss Petite closely.
"What hurt?"

"My friend told me he had read the book
From beginning to end several times.
(He had a book like mine, you know).
Then, he didn't want to learn any more lessons
So he left the book somewhere.
He only saw or spoke to the Shepherd
When he had something bothering him
Or he needed help.
It is very sad, big sheep. Very sad."

"I know what he meant, little sheep.
It hurt.
The Shepherd has been taking all these things
Out of my wool, and sometimes it hurts
When he has to pull hard;
And it especially hurts when He takes out thorns!
Some of them have gone in so deep
That I am not aware of how bad it is."

"The pain from them had dulled my senses
Over the years,
Yet when the Shepherd touched them,
They were very real!
He removed them all."

"Big sheep, you look so beautiful!
I hope you never get another hurtful thing
In your wool again.
If I see one, can I pull it out
So your wool will be kept beautiful?"

"We'll see, little sheep.
The Shepherd has a special way of pulling
These things out.
They still hurt when He pulls,
But He does it tenderly, with love."

"I'd do it with love, big sheep.
I love you, you know that."

"Little sheep, let's wait until we get to that step.
Then we'll discuss it."

"So, why are you staying in the pasture?"

M. LeGrand poured himself another cup of tea.
"Little sheep, I want to learn all I can learn
From the Shepherd while I still have time.
There is so much for Him to teach me.
While He was brushing me out
He talked to me about
Things He wants me to do
And places He wants me to visit."

"Oh, big sheep, that is marvelous," Miss Petite gasped.

That embarrassed M. LeGrand.
"I can do nothing or go anywhere yet,
Until I learn everything the Shepherd wants me to learn.
If I were to return to the flock,
I would become distracted.
Furthermore, I do not want to encounter criticism at this time.
Not so much for me as for the Shepherd.
He has been so good to me,
That I could not bear to hear sheep criticize the Shepherd."

"I know what you mean; I feel the same way.
I want to learn lessons now, even if they are hard."

"Good, little sheep. That is very wise."

"Big sheep, could you please help me?
I have been having a hard time lately.
All those days of fog made it so dreary,
And I was afraid to go out of my shelter;
Afraid of getting lost."

"Good, little sheep, you should stay home
When the fog is dense. That is sensible."

"Big sheep, would you mind if I told you
What was really bothering me?
I am excited about your wool being brushed out.
Don't think I am making little of what that meant to you,
By talking about my problems.
Please try to understand that I need to talk to you, so much."

"Go ahead, little sheep.
I knew last night that there was something troubling you.
I dared not ask. I prefer you tell me when you are ready."

"Big sheep, remember when you walked in the flock
And I was in the pasture?
I always ran back and forth
Telling you the wonderful things that
The Shepherd was teaching me.
Do you remember how excited I was
And how I couldn't talk fast enough
And so I stumbled over my tongue
Trying to get it all out?
I even pushed myself right under your nose
To get your full attention so you couldn't even eat or walk!
Remember that, big sheep?"

Of course he remembered,
But wasn't sure he wanted to go over it again.
He just didn't answer.
He waited for Miss Petite to continue.

"Big sheep, now the Shepherd
Is teaching me do's and don'ts;
Like, do have love,
Don't have jealousy, envy or strife."
"Do you know how hard it is to love?
How it hurts to love?
Not only that, but He has told me to
Prepare lessons for the tiny sheep.

He told me to write everything down
That He has taught me and continues to teach me.
Big sheep, how can I teach them
When I cannot learn them myself?"

After a long silence,
M. LeGrand nuzzled up to Miss Petite.
"Little sheep, my dear little sheep,
Did the Shepherd tell you
He wanted you to teach the tiny sheep
Or just prepare the lessons for the tiny sheep?"

"Oh! Only to prepare the lessons;
To write down everything exactly
As He has given them to me.
Make no changes, He had said.
You are right, big sheep, you are right!
I don't have to teach them.
I only have to write these things down.
I only have to record what He wants recorded;
Everything He has taught me!
Oh, you are so wonderful!"

Miss Petite leaned against M. LeGrand,
Rubbing her muzzle in his wool.
"There is such a load lifted off my shoulders.
He didn't ask me to teach.
He only told me to prepare the lessons
By writing them down."

She couldn't repeat it often enough.
The more she said it
The more she believed it and understood.
What a magnificent feeling of freedom!
She was free!
She was a free sheep again!
Why had she not understood the Shepherd?

I Shall Not Want

"Come look at my shelter, big sheep.
Don't you want to come and see
The shelter the Shepherd built for me?"

"Yes, I do. Would you show it to me?
I have admired it from afar
But you have never asked me in."

"I was hoping you'd come because you wanted to.
But it doesn't matter. You're here now."

They entered the shelter,
And Miss Petite hung the blanket back on the wall.
She remembered how, when she awakened this morning,
She had been wrapped in the purple robe,
Like the night she had saved the tiny sheep in the fog.

She took M. LeGrand to the loft,
Explaining how the Shepherd
Had placed strips of wood across the ramp
So she could pull herself up
When her legs had not worked as well as they did now.

Miss Petite reached the top of the ramp first
And her mouth fell open, aghast!
She had forgotten to take the shutters off,
And it was dark, dingy and smelled musty!
She was so embarrassed.
She wished she had never asked M. LeGrand
Up to the loft, or into the shelter at all.
M. LeGrand was right behind her.
She rushed over to the first shutter
And tried to pull it off.
It popped off and bumped her on the nose,
Then it dropped to the floor and banged her hoof.
M. LeGrand rescued her from the shutter
To prevent her from becoming battered further,
And took the other shutters down himself.

"Big sheep, I didn't intend for you to do that. I'm sorry," she whimpered.

M. LeGrand walked quietly over to her and tapped her nose.
"Shhh, little sheep. It's all right. I love you."

"Look, big sheep, look out here and see all around you!
Isn't the view amazing from this lookout?
See, we can even see the other flocks
Around the circle. Isn't it amazing?"

But M. LeGrand never answered.
He stood there, looking silently,
With tears trickling down his face.
Miss Petite wanted to ask him
What the matter was,
But instead, she knew it was best
Not to speak.
She moved close to him and snuggled.
"Big sheep, I love you very much."

"Thank you, little sheep. Thank you."

He pulled himself back together
Almost a little ashamed for showing his feelings
In front of Miss Petite.
He cleared his throat, and thanked her for
Showing him the lookout tower.
Then he muttered, "I must go now, for I have things to do.
Goodbye."

Just like that, M. LeGrand was gone
And Miss Petite was left standing alone
At the top of the ramp in the tower.

Chapter 20

A LOVE LIKE NO OTHER

For days, no, weeks,
Dark clouds hung over the sky.
Activity in the flock and the pasture
Appeared to be the same,
But there was a cold wind circling.
Few sheep sensed it,
But Miss Petite found herself
Wearing the blanket more and more.
She cleaned the inside of her shelter,
And tidied the fire pit outside.
She noticed there were hardly any leaves
Left on the tree
Where she had sat to learn lessons from the Shepherd.

Visitors came and went,
But never mentioned the chill.
Sometimes they looked with wonder
At Miss Petite bundled in her blanket.
She always had a smile
And a treat for those who dropped by.
She was thankful that Promise
Had brought by some specialties,
Because now she could share them with others.

I Shall Not Want

Miss Petite missed M. LeGrand
But knew he was learning with the Shepherd.
She thought of her friend Shadow,
And wondered if she would ever see
Where the Shepherd had taken him.

In the distance she could hear the flute playing
And waited for it to come.
Ordinarily she would have run to the flute.
She remembered the days when she scampered
In the pasture.
Now she was content to stay in her shelter.
She shivered and snuggled down in her blanket.
And always had an open fire going, day and night.

One day, as the Shepherd was making His rounds,
He came into the shelter
To sit with Miss Petite for a time.

She offered Him one of her treats
And the two sat chatting like old friends.
She realized that this had been the first time
That she and the Shepherd had eaten together,
And she was pleased.
The Shepherd didn't seem to be in too much of a hurry.
In fact, He took off His cloak and
Wrapped it around the little sheep.
Miss Petite wanted to protest
Because she already had the blanket.
She knew not to argue with the Shepherd.

Much time was spent in silence, but it was comfortable.
Finally, Miss Petite asked the Shepherd
If He would be teaching her a lesson today.
The Shepherd shook His head.
"No, little sheep. There is no need
To teach you any more lessons.
Besides, you are very tired and
Must not use up too much energy.
Little sheep, I'd like you to spend the rest of your time

Visiting with those who come to you.
You will have fewer visitors now
But they will only be sheep who need you
And sheep who come to comfort you.
The sheep who come now
Will come because I have sent them."

He continued:
"Little sheep, I want you to be careful.
You have cleaned your shelter and
The open fire pit.
Now it is time for you to enjoy
Your time as best you can.
There is no need for you to work.
When the sheep come, take time to visit with them,
But do not labor for them."

Miss Petite looked up at the Shepherd calmly,
But a tear slipped from her eye as she whispered,
"I am so cold."

"I know, little sheep, I know."

Miss Petite had a big lump in her throat and could hardly bring herself to talk.
She handed the Shepherd His book
And asked Him to read something good to her.
The Shepherd moved closer
And lay His hand on her head and read to her.
"The Lord is my shepherd;
I shall not want.
He makes me to lie down in green pastures;
He leads me beside the still waters.
He restores my soul;
He leads me in the paths of righteousness for His name's sake.
Yea, though I walk through the valley of the shadow of death,
I will fear no evil;
For You are with me;
Your rod and Your staff, they comfort me.
You prepare a table before me in the presence of my enemies:

I Shall Not Want

You anoint my head with oil;
My cup runs over.
Surely goodness and mercy shall follow me
All the days of my life;
And I will dwell in the house of the Lord
Forever." (11)

The Shepherd picked up the little sheep
And set her on the table,
Built from the lookout shutters.
Now Miss Petite could lie on the table
But still see all around.
She was delighted.
She thanked the Shepherd and
Snuggled down in her blanket, and the Shepherd's cloak.
She secretly hoped the Shepherd would not take back His cloak.
The Shepherd started down the ramp from the loft,
And waved at the little sheep.
He gently spoke to her,
"Little sheep, I will be back for you soon."

Miss Petite hoped He wouldn't wait too long
Before returning for her
For inside, she wanted to go with the Shepherd;
She was so cold.

She noticed the Shepherd had left the book open
At the same place where He had read
And so she lay repeating the words over and over.
They meant so much to her now.
She could understand that part of the book very well.
Miss Petite slept most of the time.

I Shall Not Want

I Shall Not Want

Sheep came and sheep went,
And Miss Petite recognized
Those who needed help
And those who came to comfort her.
None seemed to understand
Why Miss Petite was so cold,
But neither did they criticize.

Each day the Shepherd came to visit.
He spent more time than usual,
And talked to her without giving a lesson.
Miss Petite realized the Shepherd
Was comforting her just like the visiting sheep had done.
They had learned love from the Shepherd.
"My Dear Shepherd,
When the sheep that need me come,
I recognize them immediately
And am able to remember the lessons
You taught me and can read to them from Your book.
Some listen and some don't."

"I know, little sheep, for some have come to see Me
And have told me they had been sent by you.
I am glad. Thank you."

After a long pause,
A pause not awkward at all,
The Shepherd talked quietly to Miss Petite,
To prepare her for what was about to take place.
He told her He'd stay by her side;
That He'd give her peace,
And that she would hear angel choirs.
He told Miss Petite that she would not be alone
And would have no need to fear.
Then the Shepherd asked her if
She had any special requests.

The little sheep thought for a very long time.
"My Dear Shepherd,
I don't want to say good-bye to my friends, if You don't mind.

I Shall Not Want

We have had some good times together
And we have shared Your book and lessons.
Would You say good-bye to them for me, please?
Don't forget Miss Bow with the pink ribbon,
And thank her for being so discreet about looking after me.
She was so faithful and never told a soul what she was doing."

"And Dear Shepherd, if You wouldn't mind,
Don't forget Bumper with all the tiny sheep.
She does love You, and wants her tiny sheep to love You too.
I remember the lesson You taught me
That our minds cannot hold anything more in them
If they are filled with good;
But we must not take chances that when we are sick, weak or tired,
We don't trade off good for bad.
Dear Shepherd, I am tired now.
Will I trade off good for bad?"

"Little sheep, there is always the chance,
But while you can,
Concentrate on those words I read to you
Which you still have opened to in your book.
Also, remember,
I am only a breath away.
I am with you.
Please, little sheep, do not fret."

"And, Dear Shepherd, if You pass Miss Promise on the way,
Do ask her to come for a visit.
I have enjoyed our discussions over Your book
And have come to love her."

The Shepherd waited to see
If Miss Petite had anyone else in mind before He spoke.
Tears were flowing down the little sheep's face.
"Little sheep, I know,
You don't have to tell me.
Yes, my little one, I will do that too."

"Thank you, Dear Shepherd.
I do love You, You know that."

"Yes, my little one. I know. You have learned well."

The Shepherd paused for a moment;
"Little sheep, I have sent the big sheep on a mission.
Not for long, and not far away.
I can call him back, if you wish."

"No, Dear Shepherd, he is brushed out, and beautiful.
Thanks for letting me be part of his life.
Please don't let him get any more briars in his wool.
Please keep him clean.
He will go to You for his bells soon, I know it."

"Oh, little sheep, he has already spoken to Me
About the bells.
As soon as he is ready,
I will place them around his neck.
Little sheep, I had wanted to give you
Your tiny bell
When the big sheep received his,
But he wasn't ready to receive his earlier.
I know you are tired and weak right now,
But would you like Me to put this tiny bell
Around your neck?"

"Oh, Dear Shepherd,
That is beautiful.
It is the shiniest, the finest bell I have ever seen!
Would You please put it on for me?"

The Shepherd had already prepared
A special woven golden cord for the bell,
And He placed it around Miss Petite's neck.
It was long enough that the little sheep
Could hold it in her front legs
While lying on the table.

The Shepherd,
Pleased to see the little sheep smiling contentedly,
Left.
The little sheep played her bell
Until her legs were tired of swinging the cord.
The bell hung over the edge of the table,
And when the breeze gently blew it,
The sweetest music rang out across the pasture
And over to the other flocks of sheep.
Many did not know where the sound came from,
But a few close by recognized it
As coming from the little sheep in the lookout tower.
The music was unearthly, and all who listened,
Heard it.

Not long after the bell had started to ring,
It stopped.
Few in the pasture saw the Shepherd
Carry the little sheep home.

11. Psalm 23, Spirit Filled Life Bible, NKJV, Thomas Nelson Publishers, Inc., Nashville, TN., 1991.

Elizabeth Boyd,
1B - 275 Lower Ganges Rd
Salt Spring Island, BC
V8K 1T4